Art, Artefacts, and Chronology in Classical Archaeology

D0145799

The study of art history and archaeology depends substantially on dates which are given to artefacts and works of art. Very few students, however, have an understanding of matters of chronology or of the source material that determines the dates. In this study Professor Biers sets out to explain this crucial facet of classical scholarship.

Short introductory chapters outline the archaeology and chronology of the ancient Greek and Roman world. The core of the study is two chapters on Relative and Absolute Dating which seek, by use of specific examples, to convey the principles behind how dates are assigned to archaeological and artistic artefacts. Professor Biers presents examples from architecture, sculpture, and painting to illustrate how stylistic analysis is used to determine relative dates. Self-dating objects, such as coins, as well as the interpretation of written evidence, are explored to show how specific, absolute dates are deduced. The final chapter examines selected problems in chronology that involve the interpretation of the various kinds of evidence presented in the previous chapters.

William R. Biers is Professor of Art History and Archaeology at the University of Missouri-Columbia.

Approaching the Ancient World
Series editor: Richard Stoneman

The sources for the study of the Greek and Roman world are diffuse, diverse, and often complex, and special training is needed in order to use them to the best advantage in constructing a historical picture.

The books in this series provide an introduction to the problems and methods involved in the study of ancient history. The topics covered will range from the use of literary sources for Greek history and for Roman history, through numismatics, epigraphy, and dirt archaeology, to the use of legal evidence and of art and artefacts in chronology. There will also be books on statistical and comparative method, and on feminist approaches.

The Uses of Greek Mythology
Ken Dowden

Art, Artefacts, and Chronology in Classical Archaeology
William R. Biers

Art, Artefacts, and Chronology in Classical Archaeology

William R. Biers

London and New York

First published 1992
by Routledge
11 New Fetter Lane, London EC4P 4EE

Simultaneously published in the USA and Canada
by Routledge
a division of Routledge, Chapman and Hall Inc.
29 West 35th Street, New York, NY 10001

Typeset in 10 on 12 point Baskerville by
Selwood Systems, Midsomer Norton, Avon
Printed in Great Britain by Butler & Tanner, Frome and London

British Library Cataloguing in Publication Data
Biers, William R.
    Art, artefacts, and chronology in classical
    archaeology. – (Approaching the ancient world)
    I. Title   II. Series
    930.10285

Library of Congress Cataloging in Publication Data
Biers, William R.
    Art, artefacts, and chronology in classical archaeology/William
    R. Biers.
    p. cm.–(Approaching the ancient world)
    Outgrowth of a seminar held at the American School of Classical
    Studies in Athens during the 1989–90 academic year.
    Includes bibliographical references and index.
    1. Classical antiquities. 2. Archaeological dating–Mediterranean
    Region. I. Title. II. Series.
    DE60.B48   1992   91-45632
    938–dc20

ISBN 0–415–06318–3
        0–415–06319–1 (pbk)

Contents

Illustrations

Preface

This book grew directly out of a seminar on Greek chronology that I was privileged to direct at the American School of Classical Studies in Athens while Whitehead Visiting Professor during the 1989–1990 academic year. I had previously explored the subject of the chronology of the Greek period, at first specifically in relationship to Greek vase-painting and later more comprehensively for Greek art, in graduate seminars at the University of Missouri-Columbia, but the Athens course offered a chance to study with advanced students, many of whom had become interested in the subject of chronology in general as well as in particular problems they had encountered in their own work. Moreover, the suggested new chronology for the early Greek period propounded by E. D. Francis and Michael Vickers had reached a stage where a considerable bibliography had been built up, and the subject had reached an overall notoriety not often accorded such a seemingly dry subject. It had become popular, of course, because the question of the placement in time of individual objects, buildings, or whole sites, and their chrono-logical relationships to one another and to our own time is important, indeed basic, for the study of the ancient world. As Barbara Tuchman wrote from the point of view of an historian: "Dates may seem dull and pedantic to some, but they are fundamental because they establish sequence – what precedes and what follows – thereby leading toward an understanding of cause and effect" (*A Distant Mirror: The Calamitous 14th Century*, New York, Alfred A. Knopf, 1978, p. xv). The topic, of course, also tends to take on a certain immediacy for advanced graduate students about to launch out on their teaching careers, for they would like to be certain what to teach in this significant area! A re-examination of the evidence underlying our dating of the ancient world is also an ideal subject for a seminar for graduate students, providing insight not only into how one handles the difficult and often fractured evidence from antiquity but also as an introduction to the way scholars think – and argue.

The participants in the seminar were fortunate to hear directly from scholars who were actively involved with chronology of the early Greek period. T. Leslie Shear, Jr, the Director of the American School of Classical Studies' excavations in the Athenian Agora, took time from his busy schedule to discuss the evidence from the Agora with us. We were also honored to have Michael Vickers take part in a session, giving a presentation and then fielding, with good humor, a number of pointed questions on the subject of his proposed new chronological scheme. I remain indebted to Michael Vickers for agreeing to come to the seminar (and later suggesting that I write this book) and to the American School and its Director, William D. E. Coulson, for making his visit to Athens possible.

One of the first questions that people often raise when faced with an antiquity is "How old is it?" This is probably also one of the most frequently asked questions by students in courses that deal with the art and artefacts of antiquity (after "what's on the test?"). It is a natural question and one that is easily answered by the instructor, usually as "so many years BC," or perhaps "so many years ago." Little consideration is given on either side as to how such a deceptively precise numerical answer can be given, and this aspect of antiquity, or rather our understanding of this facet of classical antiquity, is never explored in any depth. Students usually accept dates given to them in textbooks without thinking about where the dates are derived from or on what sort of evidence they are based. An historical sense is not a characteristic of most of today's students, who can often consider as contemporary objects or actions hundreds, or sometimes even thousands, of years apart. The specifics of the ancient world are seen through a haze, or fog, depending on where one looks, and chronology can be one of the more hazy areas. Often, it is as if antiquity is being viewed through a telescope backwards; the image in the lens is tiny, only shows a portion of the scene, and there is no depth or perspective in the picture.

When one looks into the question of dates and how they are determined, one sees that all is not as cut and dried as the acceptance of a specific numerical date for a particular object or event might allow us to believe. This book is intended to provide the student and the general reader with some appreciation of the complexities and uncertainties involved in trying to assign dates to objects of art and to the artefacts of everyday use that are more commonly found in excavations in classical lands. The determination of chronology can be an involved and complex undertaking, sometimes hard to explain. I have tried to handle the difficulties involved in as direct a manner as possible in the hope that this will lead to a clearer understanding of the subject. An introductory chapter defines the discipline of classical archaeology and the types of information that can be derived from it and provides an introduction to the chronology of classical antiquity. Chapter 2 explains how the Greeks and the Romans measured and recorded the passing of time and how our own calendar developed. The following three chapters deal in some detail with the various methods of dating individual objects from the Greek and Roman world and the difficulties and uncertainties that are involved. A number of specific examples are included as illustrations of how one goes about determining dates.

It has been my goal to make this short study as useful and informative as possible. With this purpose in mind, the notes that accompany the text are usually designed to lead the reader deeper into the subject of Greek and Roman art and archaeology and the study of chronology, and they thus often contain more information than is usual in a standard reference note. The notes are also somewhat idiosyncratic in that a selected, annotated bibliography is usually provided that might not list all the possible references but does include those that I consider useful, accessible, and, in many cases, well written and easy to read. From these, the dedicated reader will be able to get back to all the necessary bibliography concerning a particular subject. Full bibliographical references to books and articles are given in the notes, so a separate bibliography has not been included. Since this work is designed primarily for English-speaking students in the broadest sense, I have tried to keep most of the references to works in English, though the occasional foreign title is to be found. A deeper penetration into any one of the topics brought up in this book will quickly indicate that classical studies is still truly an international undertaking.

A number of scholars have taken time to discuss this project with me or even to read parts of the unfinished manuscript. A simple listing of their names must suffice to convey my gratitude for their help: Jane Biers, Eugene Borza, John Camp, Eric Hostetter, Thomas Howe, Carolyn Koehler, Peter Kuniholm, Albert Leonard, Jr, Susan Rotroff, Kathleen Warner Slane. Finally, appreciation must be expressed to the editor, Richard Stoneman, and the staff of Routledge for their efficiency and patient responses to my endless questions.

Acknowledgements

The author and publishers wish to record their thanks to the following institutions and individuals who provided illustrations and/or gave permission for the use of illustrations for this work.

Alinari/Art Resource, Figures 11, 16; American School of Classical Studies at Athens, Figure 21; American School of Classical Studies at Athens, Agora Excavations, Figures 1, 4, 20, 22–4; Art Institute of Chicago, Figure 18; Susan Bird, Figure 7; The Coca-Cola Company, Figure 3; Cornell University Press, Figure 8; Alison Frantz, Figures 10, 15; German Archaeological Institute, Rome, Figures 5, 6; Hirmer Photoarchives, Figure 12; Eric Hostetter and Thomas Howe, Figure 2; Marburg/Art Resource, Figure 13; Metropolitan Museum of Art, Figures 9, 14; Museum of Art and Archaeology, University of Missouri, Figures 17, 19, 25; Susan Rotroff, Figure 26.

Chapter 1

Introduction: classical archaeology and chronology

The dictionary defines archaeology as being the scientific study of the material remains of past human activity. It is not strictly speaking a science, for its results cannot be replicated as in scientific experiments. The process of archaeology and some of its techniques can be scientific, but the discipline itself is more clearly a humanistic study in that it deals directly with material remains, the things made by humans in past times. This is one link between all the different types of archaeologies that have developed throughout the world. Whether exploring American Indian settlements in the American West, remains of medieval cities in Europe, shipwrecks under the sea, or frozen tombs in Siberia, the archaeologist concerns himself with physical remains, from the smallest objects to the largest buildings. All archaeology, as has been said, deals with physical objects and remains, and these can provide all sorts of information bearing on the life and times of the civilizations being studied; information and details not contained in any literary record that may exist. Not all this information necessarily has to come only from excavations, however. Much useful knowledge can be developed from surface surveys that seek to record and analyze remains that still exist on the surface of the ground over a specific area, looking for evidence of population density and patterns of habitation and use. Most surveying is done by topographical reconnaissance, but aerial photography has long been in use as a survey technique, joined more recently by other advanced survey methods that include geophysical investigations.[1]

Classical archaeology is that subdivision of the discipline of archaeology that concerns itself with the physical remains of the Greeks and the Romans. In one sense these two cultures can be seen as a unity, due to the strong influence of the earlier Hellenic culture on the Romans. Archaeologists tend, nevertheless, to be specialists in one culture or the other, thus mirroring the division between the Hellenist and the

Romanist that is part of our academic culture and at least partially based on whether one reads primarily Greek or Latin! Classical archaeology traditionally concerns itself with these civilizations in their literate phases, beginning in the eighth century BC and ending sometime in Late Antiquity when the Greco-Roman civilization changes into the medieval world. The material remains of these civilizations sometimes can be considered as art, more often they are everyday objects of general use, but both have a part to play in providing information about the people who made and used or admired them.

It has been observed that art history deals with the history of aesthetically pleasing objects and archaeology covers everything else. In fact, classical archaeology quite often deals with artistically pleasing objects, which is one of its more attractive features. The archaeologist who works on Greek and Roman sites is fortunate that not only are the major works of antiquity, such as architecture, sculpture, and painting pleasing to the eye, but even many of the minor everyday articles are of high quality to the modern observer. There are also, typically, a great number of objects recovered at classical sites, and the amount of material that comes out of excavations is almost overwhelming, particularly from those in the urban centers of the classical world. Most of this material consists of what has been thrown away, discarded, or hidden intentionally, or simply lost. It is practically always broken, burned, or disfigured and often fragmentary. It can be a piece of sculpture that escaped the lime kiln or a single fragment of a common drinking cup. Ancient cemeteries, on the other hand, can provide relatively intact finds that were intentionally buried to accompany the dead, and these provide scholars with direct evidence concerning the ancient funerary customs as well as providing well-preserved examples of many categories of objects. Each excavated item is a portion of an overall story, and reconstructing that story is a part of the archaeologist's job, as well as recovering the object from the earth in such a way that it is not harmed and that any evidence connected with it can be recovered and fully recorded.

Another feature of the discipline is that in the attempt to understand aspects of the ancient world from the objects, classical archaeology has the great advantage of dealing with literate civilizations, whose writings have been studied and interpreted for generations. From the time of Homer and Hesiod of the eighth century BC to Late Antiquity, a corpus of literature has been preserved that provides a great deal of information about the classical civilizations. The classical archaeologist has to fit his material into an already more or less established cultural framework. His evidence is, in one sense, direct evidence of the life of antiquity, unfiltered by an author, but the interpretation of what is found in the earth is often just as difficult, if not more so, than the decipherment and complete understanding of an obscure text.

These two positive features, the amount and quality of the archaeological material with which one deals and the wealth of literature that can be used as evidence, have also in a sense served to hold back the discipline of archaeology as it is practiced in classical lands. Archaeology in the lands around the Mediterranean started as a search for Beautiful Objects. This, together with the reliance on the ancient authors to provide cultural and historical information, perhaps led to a certain conservatism and an emphasis on organization and study of the constantly increasing mass of data derived from active fieldwork. Archaeologists in other areas, particularly in the New World, who were not bound by the traditions inherited by classical archaeology and did not have to deal with the great numbers of complex objects, developed new field techniques and new ways of interpreting the evidence derived from excavations that their colleagues in the Old World were slow to adopt. In many cases what seemed to be differences in research techniques between classical archaeology and New World archaeology were largely found to be differences in how they were described by their practitioners; however new approaches to looking at the archaeological evidence were developed and promoted by the so-called "new archaeology." Classical archaeology found itself in a position to adapt or adopt what could be useful and meaningful for itself. This has happened to a certain extent, but there is still a gap between the archaeology of the New World and classical archaeology that is only occasionally bridged. Mostly the two branches of archaeology ignore each other.

What sort of evidence can classical archaeology provide to illuminate the world of the Greeks and the Romans? As has been mentioned, the general outlines of the Greek and Roman civilizations can be determined from the study of the vast literature associated with them. The basic political, military, and social histories of Athens and Rome are recorded, as is some detail concerning the day-to-day activities of their citizens, even if the information is frequently incomplete and of varying quality in different periods and areas. We also have at least a hazy notion of their religious practices and the general way of life of some people of the period, gleaned from the literature that has survived the centuries. What archaeology does is to give breadth and context to the written sources, providing a more complete view of the ancient world than is preserved in the literary tradition through the accidents of selection and preservation. Classical archaeologists are increasingly collecting and analyzing anthropological, zoological, botanical, and geological samples in an attempt to wring the most information possible from their excavated material.

This is almost a complete contrast to the situation that exists with our knowledge of the civilizations that flourished in classical lands in the Bronze Age. These cultures are termed "prehistoric," not because they had no history, but because they flourished before written history, as we know it, existed. As a result, almost all we know of these cultures is derived from archaeology; indeed, many, such as the Minoan and Mycenaean civilizations of the Greek Bronze Age, were almost entirely unknown before the archaeologist's spade. Although the worlds of Knossos and Mycenae of prehistoric Greece were dimly reflected in later Greek myth and literature, especially in the Homeric poems, it was not until excavators began to uncover their remains that they were actually discovered to have existed. Thus, it is mainly the actual remains of these civilizations that can be used to try and recover their history and way of life. With the exception of some inscriptional evidence, which is not historical or literary and capable of varied interpretations, all that remains are the ruins of buildings and what was recovered in them together with the contents of graves. Information on the physical environment, the diet and health of the people, their activities, and other details of life can only be determined for the Bronze Age through archaeology. Of all finds, pottery is still recovered in the greatest abundance in excavations, and for non-literate civilizations, such as those in the Bronze Age, it takes on a particular importance. To a great extent, the understanding of the Greek Bronze Age, for instance, is driven by transformations detected in the development of pottery, based on observed differences in shape or decoration, and these alterations are often taken as indicative of cultural, or even political or historical, changes. Typically, an individual site, or a portion of it, is excavated, and the pottery and other finds are studied and sequences developed for that one site. Attempts are then made to synthesize the evidence with other sites of the same culture to obtain some sort of coherent understanding of the civilization concerned and its development. The disadvantage of almost complete reliance on the archaeological record, naturally, is that it precludes certain types of evidence that can be gleaned from the written record. Moreover, the interpretation of evidence derived from excavations, no matter how scientifically conducted, is tricky at best, and the field of Bronze Age archaeology is beset with differing interpretations and constantly changing versions as excavations pile up more and more information.[2]

The evidence derived from the archaeology of historic civilizations is also, of course, subject to differing interpretations, and the added dimension of attempting to integrate the archaeological evidence with what we think we know from the literary tradition adds to the difficulty in coming to a "true" understanding. This will be demonstrated in Chapter 5 in relationship to the controversies concerning the chronology of the development of art and architecture in Greece of the sixth and early fifth centuries BC. As the amount of both literary and archaeological evidence increases as one goes later in time, a clearer integration of the two types of information can be achieved, and so major difficulties are more numerous in the earlier periods than in the later ones. However, that is not to say that there are no problems even in the later periods for which there is a relatively full documentation from both sources. One of these problems concerns the ability of archaeological data to provide historical information; in other words, can history actually be written from evidence derived from archaeological investigations, given the intricacies of interpretation inherent in a field that depends on often incomplete and ambiguous evidence? Many classical archaeologists were brought up to believe that one of archaeology's goals was to add to history, and this question, a potentially vital one, has only recently been addressed. Clearly, archaeology can add to history, depending on one's definition of the term. Even the greatest skeptic would allow that archaeology has added to our knowledge of the arts, crafts, and everyday life of antiquity. Its value, however, for the interpretation, illustration, or, indeed, rec-reation of history, that can be defined in this context as the record of past events, is perhaps debatable and may be a matter of degree rather than of absolutes. However, the difficulties and uncertainties of interpret-ation are frequently not emphasized enough by those who want to be able to read a coherent story from fractured and often incomplete remains.[3]

Examples of the kinds of information classical archaeology has pro-vided are numerous. For the Greek world, for instance, excavations in the Athenian Agora, or market-place, have not only uncovered works of art and famous buildings known from our ancient sources but also artefacts and other buildings connected with the government of ancient Athens, thereby providing direct information on the workings of the administration of the ancient city. Much has been learned, for instance, about the day-to-day operations of the Athenian democracy that both illustrates and adds to the literary and historical evidence. Athens was in many ways unique in ancient Greece and not really representative of the Greek world of small, independent cities. There, archaeology has also made a contribution by investigating other smaller and perhaps more representative cities and small towns. Excavations in ancient Rome provide information about the city that was once the center of the western world, while, thanks to the preserving effects of the eruption of Vesuvius, the continuing investigations of Pompeii and Herculaneum offer a wealth of evidence concerning everyday life in smaller cities of the first century AD.[4] Archaeological work throughout the vast expanses of the Roman Empire continues to provide information on the process of Romanization and the spread of Greek and Roman culture that had such an influence on the development of western civilization as we experience it today. Distinctive Roman building types occur throughout the Empire, and synthesizing studies are beginning to provide insights into sociological, technical, geographical, and historical aspects not fully considered before.[5] Often the mere existence of archaeological remains discovered by surveys provides information. For instance, evidence derived from archaeology has been brought to bear on such subjects as land-use in Italy and the history, extent, and the military and political consequences of Rome's fortifications on the edges of her Empire.

Greek painted pottery, particularly that from Athens, found all over the Greek world, preserves scenes of myth, cult, and everyday life that add immeasurably to our understanding of Greek life.[6] Roman historical reliefs illustrate contemporary or near-contemporary historical events,[7] and even such mundane objects as oil lamps can provide information as to methods of lighting in ancient times (Figures 21–3, pp. 55–8).[8] In short, classical archaeology provides a great deal of information that can supplement and add to the rich textual tradition of the Greek and Roman world.

Excavations in classical lands have produced large numbers of finds, ranging from complete pots to unidentifiable scraps of pottery and metal to architectural remains, and even occasionally whole statues or wall paintings. The following chapters are concerned with how these individual fragments of a past world are dated; in other words, how their relationship in time to our own period is determined, and this is, of course, connected to the general questions of chronology and how it is determined. There are two ways of asserting the date of an object derived from an excavation, providing it has a recognizable form and enough is preserved to make sense of it. One of these sees it in relationship to other objects of the same kind made either before or after it. This is termed a "relative chronology," for it dates the object in relation to other objects and assigns it a "relative date." This is useful for an understanding of how objects develop over time, but not sufficient, since it does not relate the article to our own time, that is, it does not tell us how old it is, which is one of the first questions that is asked about any object from the ancient world. Since our method of time reckoning employs the year, the object must be placed within this framework and given a "date" of so many years BC or AD, or so many years before the present, usually expressed as "so many years ago." The object then is not related to other objects of the same type but to an absolute scale, and this is known as "absolute chronology," the object being given an "absolute date."Any find can be dated either relatively or absolutely, or *both* relatively and absolutely, and the following chapters outline how this is done.

This chapter concludes with a simplified table of dates for general reference:

Greece

Bronze Age	3000–1100 BC
Dark Ages	1100–900 BC
Geometric and Orientalizing periods	900–600 BC
Archaic period	600–480 BC
Classical period	480–323 BC
Hellenistic period	323–31 BC

Rome

Republican period	509–27 BC
Julio-Claudian period	27 BC–AD 68
Flavian period	AD 69–96
Trajan–Hadrian	AD 98–138
Antonine period	AD 138–193
Severan period	AD 193–235
Tetrarchic period	AD 284–312
Constantine	AD 312–336
"Late Roman"	AD 395–mid seventh century

These dates are only approximate but represent a general agreement on the part of scholars as to the overall dates for the various periods listed. These periods are more or less a modern creation, rendered according to the time-scale in use today and made up from art historical or historical evidence, some of which is debatable. Many of the dates are conventional, such as the end of the Archaic period at the time of the Persian invasion in 480 BC and the death of Alexander the Great marking the beginning of the Hellenistic period in 323 BC; they bear little relation to reality, which did not arrange itself into such neat divisions. It must be emphasized that these modern divisions of the material are only generally applicable and that the numerical dates offer a precision not observable in real life.

Chapter 2

How time is recorded

The alternation of light and dark that forms day and night, the apparent movement of the sun in the sky, the waxing and waning of the moon, and the movement of the stars – all these natural phenomena were observed by ancient peoples. The concept of time – that something happened before or after something else – and the realization of its relation to changes in the natural habitat caused by the seasons must have developed quickly in the primitive mind. All ancient civilizations measured time based on these principles.[1]

In our own time a "day" contains periods of dark and light and begins at "midnight," which falls during the period of darkness. In ancient times the perceived transit of the sun across the sky generally defined the unit of time known as a "day." The division of the cycle of dark and light into twenty-four hours was already known in Egypt before 2000 BC, with ten hours of light, two of twilight, and twelve night-time hours. This changed to a simpler system, generally used by the Greeks and the Romans, in which there were twelve light and twelve dark hours. The division of the working day into twelve equal hours took no account of the time of year even though daylight hours were actually longer in summer than in winter. This does not seem to have posed any special problems in civilizations perhaps less concerned with exactness in keeping time than we are. Astronomers adapted the division of the whole light–dark cycle into twenty-four constant units and further divided each hour into sixty equal units. Time was determined by observing the position of the sun during the day or the stars at night. During the day sundials could be used and water-clocks were available at night or on cloudy days.

Sundials are very ancient instruments, and a number are known from Greek and Roman times. They all consist basically of two parts, a pointer and a dial on which the hours of the day are marked. The shadow cast by the pointer moves across the dial as the sun appears to cross the sky, and the time can be read directly from the grid that represents the hours. The most common type has a concave face and a pointer and was designed to point south. Each sundial needed to be set for the correct latitude and then could be so constructed that the shadow would pass along the appropriate sets of lines for the various seasons. Truly elaborate sundials bore signs of the zodiac in the appropriate positions and perhaps notations as to typical events or happenings at particular times. Sundials range in size from small traveling examples, which had movable dials that could be set for varying latitudes, to a truly gigantic one erected in Rome by the Emperor Augustus in 9 BC. Its pointer was an Egyptian obelisk and its dial, engraved on a pavement, covered an area measuring approximately 165 by 75 meters.[2]

Water-clocks (known in Greek as *klepsydras* or "water thieves") also came in various sizes and shapes. A simple type was used in the law courts of Athens in which water flowed from one container into another through a spout in the upper vessel. In a fifth-century BC example found in the Athenian Agora, it took about 6 minutes for the water to flow completely into the lower container; presumably this was the length of time allowed for a speech. Larger, architecturally elaborated water-clocks served the community and civic functions. There are basically two types of water-clocks, the out-flow and the in-flow. The out-flow clock consists of a tank of water with an outlet at its base. Water is poured into the tank and escapes from the outlet. As it does so, the water level lowers and a pointer attached to a float moves down a scale that is time calibrated. Problems with this design are that the water-level will sink more quickly at the beginning when the tank is full than at the end when the vertical pressure is less and that different scales need to be used at times of the year when the hours vary in length. An in-flow water-clock avoids this by measuring time through rising rather than falling water. A float with a pointer would then rise up along a vertical scale. Another tank acts as a reservoir, providing stable pressure by being continually filled to an overflow point. The rate of flow of water from the reservoir to the clock could be controlled so that, for instance, the tank containing the pointer could be filled more slowly in the summer when the daylight hours were longer. This arrangement also allowed the use of a single, fixed scale. We hear from the ancient sources of additional dials that showed the heavens, and of numerous gadgets worked by water or air pressure that could be attached to in-flow water-clocks. It is probable that quite elaborate time-telling devices may have been in use by the Hellenistic period.[3]

Various calendars were devised to measure and record time. Each city state in Greece had its own calendar with distinctive, local names for the months, and these differed from state to state. The Greeks used the lunar phases for measuring time for civil calendars, beginning the month at the time of the new crescent moon. The problem of a calendar based on the moon, however, is that the solar year of 365 $\frac{1}{4}$ days is longer than twelve moon months (or lunations) by about eleven days and eighteen days shorter than the thirteen moon months. A twelve-month calendar based on lunations would then fall behind the solar year so that celebrations originally falling in one season could easily eventually occur in a completely different season. Thus, in order to adjust the lunar year (which is itself not constant) so that the seasons will coincide with the appropriate months, days had to be added to months in the lunar calendar to keep it in tune. This is known as intercalation. Since it is only practical to intercalate whole units, such as days or, more commonly months, an excess of time each year is usually accumulated, and this over the centuries will result in the lunar year getting ahead of astronomical reality, necessitating further adjustments as apparently happened continually in antiquity and again, much later, in the sixteenth century (see below, pp. 15–16).

Several calendars were in use simultaneously in Athens in the Classical period. There was a lunar year controlled by the observation of the moon, which was divided into twelve months with an extra month added from time to time to keep it together with the seasons. There was also a civil calendar based on annually changing archons (magistrates) so that a document could indicate both an archon's name and a month designation. A list of archons has come down to us, and many of the archon years can be attributed from it to specific years in our own calendar. A third calendar was connected with the period in office of the Prytaneis, the executive committee of the Boule, or council. Each Prytaneis was made up of fifty men chosen from each of the ten tribes in rotation. Their duty was to see to the day-to-day administration of the city from their headquarters in a building in the market-place or Agora. A contingent of the committee even dined and slept there in order to provide an immediate response should any emergency arise. Each Prytaneis served for thirty-five or thirty-six days, which allowed a total time of 365 days for the ten committees. The relationship of these three different calendars, the methods used for adjusting or changing them for various reasons, including adjustments to the solar year, are beyond the scope of this book.[4]

Other cities also used the period in office of a magistrate of one sort or another as a basis for their calendars. In addition, sometimes dates were expressed in relationship to the term in office of a religious official. These various different methods of dating events all apparently coexisted together, and often writers use more than one reference to the time of a particular event, which is important for trying to relate the various systems to one another. The careful historian, Thucydides, for example, fixes the start of the Peloponnesian War in reference to three different systems of dating currently in use in three of the most powerful states of the time. He records that the war began when Chrysis was in her forty-eighth year as priestess of Hera at Argos, when Ainesias was ephor (magistrate) at Sparta, and when Pythodorus was archon at Athens.[5]

We should not be surprised by the seemingly chaotic character of Greek time-reckoning, in which a number of calendars and methods of telling time were in use at the same time. Even in our own time one calendar is in use, yet we routinely speak of a fiscal year, an academic year, and a church or liturgical year. In ancient times, as now, the average citizen lived mainly by one calendar, and if the days of religious festivals, for instance, were variable each year, as Easter is today, it made little difference to his daily life.

Systems referring to numbers of years also existed in the Greek world. Probably the earliest was the use of generations to measure time. This system can be found in the works of a number of ancient writers, who construct a relative time sequence with reference to the length of the lives of successive individuals. The problem with this type of chronology for the modern investigator is to discover how many years make up a generation. The length of a generation appears to vary with different writers, and even individual authors are often inconsistent in their use of generational reckoning. There does not seem to be an agreed number of years that can be considered a "generation," and estimates by modern scholars can vary between thirty-three and forty years for a generation depending on the author involved or the interpretation of an author's use of the term.

Eras, periods of time initiated by some particular event, were often established by the accession to power of a particular individual, and dating by the rulers of one kind or another had a long history in the civilizations of western Asia. "In the X year of the reign of so and so" was a common formula in use in the Greek East. Occasionally, eras could also be initiated by some important historical, religious, military, or political event, such as the renaming of a city or the date of the beginning of Roman rule. Shorter periods could also be used for determining dates. By the fourth century AD many local documents in the Roman Empire were dated in terms of taxation cycles of fifteen years.[6]

One of the most widely used systems was employed in the Greek-speaking land of western Asia Minor well into the Roman period. This era began on the date King Seleucus became governor of Babylon. This year can be calculated to be 312/311 BC in our modern system, and this, then, is year one of the Seleucid era. Each year of this era began officially in the late summer or early autumn and hence overlaps two of our years. Numerous inscriptions from this part of the ancient world bear dates expressed in this system. A typical example on a funerary monument below a sculptured bust of a woman reads "Levitha, brave, carefree, farewell. Year 408." Calculation reveals that the Seleucid era date of 408 equals the date AD 97/98 in our calendar.[7] Thus the specific date indicates when the sculpture was carved almost to the year. It also provides a date at which the particular forms of the letters of the inscription were in use. In general, dated inscriptions of this kind provide chronological fixed points for funerary monuments in this part of Syria, for sculpture, and also for inscriptions. For the definition of the term "fixed point," see Chapter 3.

The confusion of each city having a different calendar that is often based on local considerations led to attempts in antiquity to produce universal eras that could be valid across the board and might be used by writers who sought to place in a chronological framework events that occurred in the distant past. The most famous of these was the list of Olympic victors, traditionally drawn up by a certain Hippias of Elis in the fifth century BC. Since the Olympic Games occurred in four-year cycles beginning traditionally in 776 BC, the lists supply a chronological framework in which particular events can be placed.[8] In theory this should work, since Olympic year 1.1 equalled 776 BC, and most ancient historians used Olympiads from the time of Eratosthenes (third to second century BC) on; year one of the Seleucid era was equated, for instance, with Olympic year 117.1. The chronology based on the Olympic festivals formed a closed system, and the main problem is relating it to other chronologies that did not date by Olympiads. An additional problem is its own internal integrity, especially for the early periods, and doubts about its veracity before the fifth century BC had been voiced even in antiquity. The philosopher and biographer Plutarch, probably writing in the early second century AD, openly states that the Olympic lists established by Hippias of Elis rested on no definite evidence.[9]

Julius Caesar's calendar that was instituted in 46 BC is essentially the basis of our calendar today. It contained twelve months making up 365 days and provided for one day to be intercalated every four years to attain the necessary $365\frac{1}{4}$ days. This calendar replaced that in use under the Republic, which may have had only ten months, but our knowledge of the early calendar of Rome is still faulty. It seems, however, from the dating of known eclipses, that the calendar in the second century BC had become badly out of synchronization with the solar year. The historian Livy recorded an eclipse that occurred before the battle of Pydna in 186 BC as taking place on September 3. Astronomical calculations indicate that it actually happened on June 21, so the civil calendar at that point must have been out some two-and-a-half months in relation to the solar year.[10] The Julian calendar, after some initial adjustment under Augustus, spread slowly throughout the Roman Empire, but local calendars continued to be used in many places, even after the new calendar was introduced.

Apart from a calendar adjusted to agree with the seasons, the Romans also used other methods of recording time for civil purposes, for instance dating by magistrates in the same way as the Athenians recorded events by reference to their archon lists. Lists of consuls, the *fasti consulares*, have come down to us and provide names of these magistrates from the founding of the Republic in 509 BC well into the sixth century AD. The lists are generally considered as reliable at least from about 300 BC; our versions were published during the reign of Augustus.

Events of various types could also be described as "so many years from the founding of the city" (*ab urbe condita* – often abbreviated in modern works as "AUC"). The actual date of the founding of Rome, however, was disputed, varying for most authorities between 759 and 748 BC. In the Augustan lists of consuls the date works out to 752 BC. The most commonly accepted date, however, was that of 753 BC, popularized by the Roman writer of the first century BC, Terentius Varro, and related by many to the Olympic year 6.3.

The Julian calendar was generally used for civil functions in the Roman Empire, and at the Council of Nicaea (AD 325) the Christian church accepted that calendar for ecclesiastical reckoning. A major change was made in the sixth century with the invention of the BC/AD system familiar to us. In the early years of the century the eastern and western churches were divided as to when to celebrate Easter. A monk by the name of Dionysius Exiguus was asked to compile a new table, which he based on a chronological cycle in use in Alexandria, Egypt. He listed dates up to AD 626, and chose as a set point of departure the date of the birth of Christ, which he fixed, following other calculators, in the *Roman* year 753 (*ab urbe condita*), i.e., 753 years after the founding of the city of Rome according to the chronology of Varro and others. All following years to our time and beyond are then expressed as "year of the Lord" (Anno Domini, or AD). Years before the birth of Christ are expressed as "before Christ" or BC. Years after Christ begin with AD 1 and count forwards; years BC start with the year 1 BC (there is no "0" year) and run backward into the past becoming higher as the dates are earlier. So, 10 BC is earlier by nine years than 1 BC. In expressing a span of dates "before Christ" it is necessary to go from numerically higher numbers to lower ones, so that the third quarter of the fifth century BC is expressed as 450–425 BC. Another point to be remembered is that the year dates within centuries are multiples of the lowest date, i.e. the fourth century BC is 400–300 BC, and dates within the fourth century are in the 300s not the 400s, i.e., the middle year of the fourth century is 350 BC. This is, of course, also true for dates after Christ; our twentieth-century dates are in the 1900s and the midpoint of the twentieth century AD was 1950.

The BC/AD convention has been considered internally inconsistent and clumsy, and a number of alternatives have met with varying degrees of acceptance. The term "before the Christian Era (BCE)" is often substituted for "before Christ (BC)." The abbreviation "BCE" is also used by Jewish writers when expressing "BC" dates in the Christian calendar and stands for "before the common era." "In the Hebrew year (AH [Anno Hebraico])" is also occasionally found. "Before present (BP)" occurs in some scientific writing, and "the present" is defined by convention as AD 1950. "Christian Era (CE)" or "after Christ (AC)" refer to dates after the birth of Christ and the term "Common Era (CE)" is also used by Jewish writers on analogy with their use of "BCE."

Church scholars have placed the birth of Christ several years earlier than did Dionysius Exiguus on the basis of evidence concerning the death of Herod, but this has had no effect on the accepted convention of the dating of the Christian era. The calendar did have to undergo a further correction, however. The intercalation of one day in four years in the Julian calendar led it to become longer than a year measured by the seasons, and a major reform by Pope Gregory XIII in 1582 sought to correct this by removing ten days and making adjustments in the method of intercalation to reduce the number of days added over time. The Gregorian calendar is in use in most of the world today, but it was not adopted for political reasons in England and the American colonies until 1752, when it was necessary to drop eleven days. This caused some unrest at the time, with crowds shouting: "Give us back our eleven days!" The new calendar was said to be "New Style," while dates in the Julian calendar were referred to as "Old Style." Documents in the eighteenth century often give dates in both the New Style (NS) and the Old Style (OS). The Gregorian calendar also regularized the beginning of the year at January 1. Prior to its adoption it had been placed by various nations at December 25, January 1, or March 25 (as in England before 1752).[11]

The recording and measurement of time has been a preoccupation of a great number of people in many different parts of the world, and the passage of time remains to this day at the center of human consciousness. Only the bare outlines of the development of the western tradition of measuring the passing of time could be recounted here. This method is in use in most of the modern world and provides a workable way to indicate the movement of events and their temporal relationships to one another. The problems involved in relating objects made by humans in the past to our own time is somewhat different from the measurement of the days or the progression of the seasons. The age of an object must be established in relationship to the present by both relative and absolute means, and these different approaches are outlined in the following chapters.

Chapter 3

Relative dating

The development of the study of fluvial geology in the nineteenth century led to the recognition that earth can be observed to have been laid down in sequences of layers, or strata, piled one above the other. When animal bones and human implements of different types were observed in various strata at different depths, the understanding developed that the upper strata were likely to have been laid down after the lower ones and were therefore likely to be younger in time. The concept of stratification, that the deeper one goes into the earth, the earlier will be the material found in the superimposed strata, is the basis of all land archaeology and was first probably regularized by Worsaae in Denmark in the 1880s. The idea, however, had been recognized occasionally earlier, notably by the polymath Thomas Jefferson in his *Notes on the State of Virginia* in 1784.[1]

The stratification observable in excavations is derived from decay, abandonment, or destruction. A city or a town once a thriving entity can disappear over the centuries so that its very location is forgotten, and nothing observable marks its position. Buildings and streets can be covered up and disappear beneath the earth. How does this happen?

An abandoned building will eventually fall down, and its constituent components return to nature, assuming they are not artificial. This is particularly true for the ancient world in which most buildings, until the widespread use of Roman concrete, were built of perishable materials such as wood or mudbrick, which can disappear almost without a trace. Even major buildings built of cut and shaped stone can provide building material for later generations and as a result be completely quarried away. The normal erosion of the soil, particularly from hills and mountains, will quickly bury a wall, and years of rain and wind-borne earth causes revegetation to occur, which accumulates layers of humus over the remains, burying them further. Such specific events as the shifting of river beds, or sinking of a coastline, also contribute to the disappearance of ancient remains. In ancient times, with the use of wood, mudbrick, and stones, a building quickly becomes a mound of debris, which may be pillaged for useful material, leveled, and built upon again. In this way mounds are built, familiar from excavations in the Near East. Even in towns that have a continual habitation over a number of years, buildings are rebuilt and added to from time to time. Dirt floors are renewed, internal walls are torn down, or new ones are built, rubbish is swept into the street, which rises over the years relative to the buildings on each side of it. Changing population patterns or other circumstances cause population shifts, which lead people to leave their homes to settle elsewhere, and nature takes over, eventually burying the buildings.

A dramatic event, such as a fire, earthquake, or destruction in war can destroy a town and bury it in its own debris. It may be reinhabited by its former citizens or by others, maybe even by its own destroyers. The event may be traceable archaeologically by the discovery of architectural remains superimposed on top of the earlier buildings. The later constructions are often built differently or laid out on a new orientation. Traces of violent destruction may indicate a known historical event, but without the excavation of an entire city, it is difficult to determine the difference between a single event, such as a building burning down from a chance fire, and an historical city-wide event such as a sack. A site such as Akrotiri on the island of Thera in the Mediterranean north of Crete is an example of a specific area being overwhelmed by a single event or series of events, in this case the eruption and subsequent explosion about the middle of the second millennium BC, or slightly earlier, of a volcano that had constituted a large portion of the island. The events of AD 79 are familiar, and Pompeii, Herculaneum, and the other sites around the Bay of Naples provide another and better documented example of destruction and entombment as the result of a natural disaster, in this case the eruption of the volcano Vesuvius.[2] Earthquakes also cause their share of destruction, and a number of destruction levels found in archaeological excavations clearly can be attached to earthquake activity, although it is often tempting when faced with evidence for massive destruction to cite otherwise undocumented seismic activity as an explanation for it.

Excavation technique is primarily based on stratigraphy, with a general rule that can be expressed as "last in, first out." Humans dig into the ground, to make foundations, store things, get rid of rubbish, look for water, etc., and each of these intrusions can extend into lower, earlier strata. Hence, archaeological practice is to remove these intrusions first so as not to mix material from such an intrusion with the earlier finds in the surrounding fill. This is fine in principle but often difficult to do in practice, especially when working with earth fills and subtle changes in color or consistency. Earth records its own disturbances by changes in composition, texture, color, consistency, or a combination of these characteristics. A softness, for instance, will exist where the ancient layers have been dug up and then refilled. A competent pickman can find these changes by the feel and appearances of the soil as he picks through it, but involved areas with many intrusions and a complicated history of human use may frustrate and deceive even the most experienced excavator.

Strata can be dated, relative to one another, and occasionally absolutely, by the latest objects found within them. Thus, an object found in a layer below a similar object found higher up can generally be considered the earlier artefact. This is not invariably the case, for occasionally what is known as "reverse stratigraphy" is encountered in which later objects are found actually below earlier ones. This may have resulted from some major disturbance in the earth brought about by human activity, although a single, small object can often move around within the earth to an amazing extent. Small, heavy objects, like coins, often sink due to their own weight, especially in loosely compacted soils, and some burrowing animals are known to collect small, usually shiny, objects, often transporting them well beyond their original place of deposition, thus providing an example of reverse stratigraphy by bringing a later object to a nest well below in an earlier stratum. Major cases of reverse stratigraphy often occur as a result of ancient building activity when soil from elsewhere is brought in for filling, leveling, or construction. An example of this would be, for instance, the construction of a Roman terrace to support a new temple built on the site of an earlier building, say of the Hellenistic period. The Roman contractor brings in earth that has Bronze Age sherds in it, which is dumped on top of the Hellenistic remains to make the terrace. A future excavator of the site would then find Bronze Age material stratified above Hellenistic remains! This, of course, is an obvious example and easily recognizable in the field, but more subtle examples of reverse stratigraphy are hard to detect and often cause difficulties. Earth brought in from elsewhere that has archaeological material in it may mislead an excavator into thinking that the stratum or construction in which this soil lies dates from the period of the material found in the earth. Mounds made for burials by heaping up earth containing artefacts earlier than the period of their construction could mislead an investigator who might initially only find the earlier evidence. Schliemann found only prehistoric pottery in a large mound on the plain at Marathon that later yielded bones, ashes, and pottery usually considered to belong to the burial of the Athenian dead from the battle of Marathon in 490 BC.[3]

Often objects are found in what is known as a "closed" or "sealed deposit," in other words, an undisturbed deposit completely separate from any possible intrusion. An example of a sealed deposit could be a buried pot containing coins, or a stratum completely sealed by an impervious upper level, such as a Roman concrete floor. In the latter case, anything found under this floor would presumably have been made earlier than the floor or at least cannot be later than it. Therefore, anything found on the floor or in habitation levels immediately above it must be later in date than the material sealed under the floor. Two Latin phrases are often used in relation to deposits in which dated material is found. They are *terminus post quem* (limit after which) and *terminus ante quem* (limit before which). In the example just cited of a sealed deposit, an object under the floor would have a *terminus ante quem* of the date of the floor, since it could not have been deposited after the floor sealed the deposit. This says nothing about the absolute date of the object; it could have been made at any time *before* the floor was laid. The contents of the deposit could be very mixed with a number of objects produced well before the deposit was closed. Since dating is done on the basis of the latest datable object in a given stratum, much earlier objects in the level do not affect the chronology except to give a possible indication of length of time. In most cases objects considerably earlier than the latest objects in a deposit are considered simply to have been old before they were buried and are known as "heirlooms." This mixing of old and new material is not all that unusual, but when the earlier objects are in abundance there is always the possibility that the later objects may be intrusions from a higher level, perhaps brought in by unrecognized disturbances into the lower levels, as can certainly happen in an area with complicated stratigraphy (as an example, Figure 1) or even by burrowing animals, who are sometimes the culprits in these cases, as has been mentioned.

Conversely, objects found above or even on the hypothetical floor would have the floor as a *terminus post quem*, meaning that they have to have been deposited after the floor was constructed, although many of them could in fact have been made before the floor was laid. Finding a dated object, such as a coin, within a floor would provide a relative date for that floor (any time after the coin was minted, the date of the coin then being the *terminus post quem* for the floor). Although these Latin expressions are commonly used in archaeological reports, they are clumsy

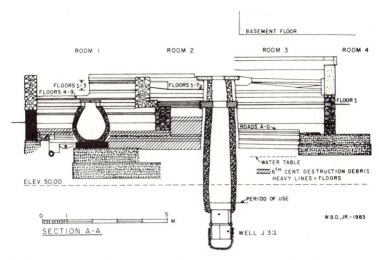

Figure 1   Athenian Agora. Vertical cross section of medieval levels

and often open to confusion, especially for the non-expert reader. However, they have become an accepted shorthand method of expressing relative chronological relationships.

The complicated nature of the stratigraphy encountered in an urban site, such as Athens, is shown in Figure 1, which is a section drawing through the medieval levels (approximately the ninth to the eleventh centuries) in an area of the Athenian Agora.[4] Drawings of vertical sections of a site, together with horizontal ground plans of remains at various levels, are a common method to show how various levels and features are related to one another. In section drawings, the view is a vertical one, almost like a slice of cake, with the different floors, levels, architectural features, and intrusions shown in relationship to each other. This particular drawing clearly illustrates the problems of reuse of an area by successive generations of inhabitants who continually rebuilt and reordered their living spaces. What is illustrated is a section looking east through several rooms of medieval houses that were found below modern levels, indicated by the basement floor of a modern (probably nineteenth-century) building at the upper right, and above the remains of the ancient city in this portion of the Agora. Their hard clay floors were renewed, and their walls were rebuilt, changed, and reoriented during three major architectural phases representing some 200 years of continuous occupation. Different rooms show different sequences of levels, and their

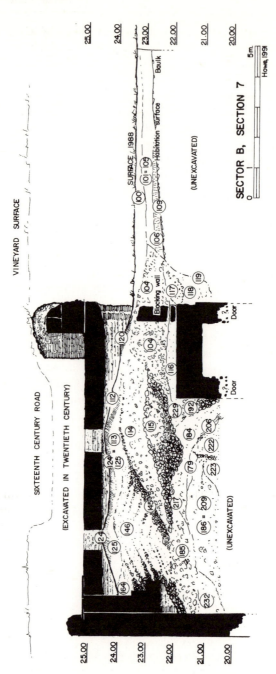

Figure 2 Rome, Palatine Hill excavations. Section through standing Roman vault and associated levels, drawn by Thomas Howe

relationship to one another is not always clear. Buildings of the Greek period, in this area well below the ground level of the houses, were pillaged by the inhabitants of medieval Athens for building material and even as foundations for their own constructions: note the large storage pot, or pithos, used from an upper level, which was set down on a pre-existing step of a fifth-century BC building, and later walls using the large rectangular blocks of ancient Greek buildings as foundations. As the ground level rose, and new floors were laid, the pithos had to be provided with a raised collar so that it could still be used. A well in the courtyard of a house penetrates far into earlier levels and shows two periods, the original shaft having been filled up after some possible damage and rebuilding to the structure. After some time there was another recon-struction, and the well was cleaned out and put back into use. Its well-head now was almost a meter above its old setting and was in fact raised in the reconstruction from its original location. This drawing is simplified for publication, working sections used in the excavation would show more distinctly the various different floor levels in greater detail and larger scale, but it clearly indicates the complex and difficult stratigraphy that confronts an excavator in an area such as this. The constant activity over the centuries and the large number of intrusions into earlier strata with the possibilities of contamination that they provide make analysis of the area quite difficult. Since chronology depends on the relationship of the finds from the various strata, understanding the stratigraphy and how the various features, levels, and fills relate to one another is a major goal.

Figure 2 shows a section from an excavation currently (1991) in progress at the foot of the north-east corner of the Palatine Hill in Rome. It illustrates the problems involved in excavating a great depth of accumulated earth and debris around and within the standing remains of an ancient building.[5] The view is to the west with the north to the right, and shows a standing Roman masonry vault that is probably part of the substructure of a hall belonging to a third-century building complex. It is deeply buried by erosion and grading from the hill and was completely covered by the sixteenth century, when it was under a road and a vineyard. The whole area was dug away at various times from the 1930s through the 1960s, re-exposing the Roman building down to the level of the "1988 surface" on the exterior to the north. As can be seen from the section, excavation has not yet reached the ancient ground surface that went with the building on the exterior, nor the floor of the room under the vault. Here the excavators have just come upon the lintels of two doors and conjecture that the floor may lie another 2

Figure 3   Development of the Coca-Cola bottle, 1894–1956

meters below. The complicated layers of debris within the structure indicate that some of the filling was deposited in the room through holes in the vault, probably when the building was buried at the time the hill was graded for the vineyard. Other strata may belong to a late reuse of the building that is indicated by the discovery of a rough blocking wall, largely built of reused material, in the north opening of the vault, but further study of these layers and the material found in them should clarify the archaeological history of the room. This area was also not immune to intrusions from above, as can be seen in the robbing cut, labelled "119," on the outside of the building.

Vertical sections, such as this one, made as the digging proceeds, provide a record of the various levels and features as they are dug through. In a sense, archaeology is destruction, for upper levels must be removed to expose earlier remains, and careful recording during this process can help the archaeologist to comprehend the area. Often an excavator does not recognize what is being found as work proceeds, and full understanding only comes later, after careful study of the finds and the excavation records.

Excavation uncovers things as well as structural features and disturbances in the strata, and objects made by humans, both those that can be considered "art" and those that are not, tend to change over time. This change can be in shape, type, or method of decoration, technique of manufacture, or combinations of these traits. The particularly characteristic or distinctive way an object appears to the eye can be said to be its style. A change in its appearance, or details of its appearance, or attributes, is seen to be a stylistic change or development. Stylistic change can be related to time, but is not necessarily always caused by the passage of time, and can be slow or almost nonexistent, depending on a variety of factors. Objects of everyday use, such as common tools, change their shape slowly, for once a tool can do a job there is little reason to alter the shape, and many useful objects, such as hand-farming implements or fish-hooks, have remained the same shape today as they were in antiquity. Roman dice are identical in shape to those rolled today.

Although the concept of stylistic change may seem odd, it is something with which we live and which we recognize daily without being aware of what we are doing. Whenever we can tell the difference in appearance between two objects of the same type, we are observing stylistic change, whether it be between automobiles made several years apart or between styles of clothing. When we say something looks "old fashioned," we are recognizing stylistic change over time. These changes can happen for a variety of reasons; changes of taste or fashion, technical improvements or inventions that allow changes not possible in the past, a change in population, evolving societal needs, or even the genius of an individual inventor or artist. A stylistic change can be rapid or not, obvious or subtle, but it is a fact of life that styles change.

Objects can be placed in sequence or ordered on the basis of their changes in style, providing what appears to be an evolutionary development. This is true even in modern times when as common an object as a soft drink bottle has recognizable changes in shape and decoration over approximately 100 years (Figure 3). Analysis of the sequence of bottles shows that such things as shape and proportion of the bottle, color of the glass, method of decoration, and its composition all changed throughout time from the earliest example, made in 1894, to the bottle type that appeared in 1956, and which is still familiar today.

An evolutionary way of viewing stylistic development is common for ancient art, and is perhaps an influence from the natural world in which biological principles of birth, growth, and death can be observed. Change of style in objects, however, does not always show evolution in a biological sense, for it can be influenced by many factors, as has been mentioned above. If a given object looks different from other objects of its type, it might not necessarily be because it is younger or older. Often objects of the same type made at the same time but in different parts of the ancient world differ considerably from one another. This can be for a variety of reasons, including intentional copying or local adaptation of imported objects, provincialism, lack of ability, or even the desire to produce an object whose shape is readily identifiable as coming from a particular place or perhaps containing a specific substance. The varied shapes of contemporary clay transport amphoras provide an example of this last reason. These large pots were the shipping containers of their day, being carried throughout the ancient world, holding a variety of contents. Those shown in Figure 4 were all found in destruction debris datable to the sack of Athens by the Roman general Sulla in 86 BC. Each example comes from a different place in the Mediterranean world of the Late Hellenistic period (from the left, Rhodes, Knidos, and Chios; the amphora on the right is a Roman shape), and they clearly differ from one another in proportion, placement and shape of handles, treatment of lip, etc. These differences in shape would clearly announce their origins to contemporary consumers, in much the same way that a modern Bordeaux bottle differs in shape from a Burgundy bottle. In this case shape difference is not a function of the passage of time.

Change and development of style in sculpture, for instance, can also

Figure 4   Hellenistic amphoras from the Sullan destruction levels in the Athenian Agora. The fifth-century BC Temple of Hephaistos is in the background

be affected by what might be called the "problem of generations." Artists of different ages and levels of artistic quality are usually active at the same time. Thus, very differing styles may be encountered that are not different from one another because of date, but because they are the work of older, less competent, or less active artists. Quality also has something to do with the analysis of style, especially when it comes to art, but there are dangers when it comes to assessing quality in relationship to chronology. Poorly made statues, for instance, might wrongly be thought closer to the beginning of a stylistic series, for their relatively undeveloped nature can be mistaken for early stages of a style's development.

An example of great stylistic divergences in art created at approxi-

Figure 5   Detail from the fourth spiral of Trajan's Column showing a charging Roman cavalryman

mately the same time but widely separated in space and quality can be seen in Figures 5 and 6. Historical relief is a typically Roman art form, and one of the prime examples of this genre is to be found on the famous Trajan's Column, dedicated by the emperor in Rome in AD 117. Carved on this monumental triumphal monument are scenes representing Trajan's campaigns in Dacia, that part of Europe that today corresponds, more or less, to modern Rumania. The scenes are rendered in a continuing spiral from bottom to top and illustrate, in an almost documentary style, actions and incidents that apparently actually occurred in the course of the campaign. Figure 5 shows an excerpt from the fourth spiral where the sculptural quality and wealth of detail can be appreciated in a scene that records Roman cavalry riding to the attack. Although the

Figure 6   Carved slab with a charging horseman in relief from the Tropaeum Triani, Adamklissi, Rumania

proportions of the rider and the horse are not true to life, the modeling of the horse's musculature and the treatment of the rider's body and clothing show a masterful handling of the subject of a charging horseman. The sculpture on the column, as an official monument, shows the quality of work that could be produced in the capital.

Figure 6 illustrates a carved slab that originally decorated a great trophy monument set up in Dacia itself, the Tropaeum Traiani ("Trajan's Trophy") at Adamklissi in Rumania. The monument was built in the form of a circular drum supporting an hexagonal tower that served as a base for a trophy in the form of tree trunk on which was hung a cuirass and other military equipment. The tower bore an inscription which gave the name of the Emperor Trajan. Fifty-four slabs, approximately 5 feet by 4 feet (1.52 meters by 1.22 meters) in size, decorated the drum, and most scholars connect the scenes of war depicted on them with the Dacian campaigns. The scene illustrated here is of another charging horseman, probably a Roman auxiliary wearing chain-mail, and should be compared to the equestrian figure from the monument in Rome. Here the proportions, flatness of carving, lack of detail, and crudity of rendering clearly indicate a provincial work, far removed from a major monument erected in the imperial capital by artists of greater ability. There is a similar lack of proportion between horse and rider, but the attention to detail and the sculptural quality of the example from Rome emphasizes the difference between the two similar scenes.[6]

The two monuments, Trajan's Column and the Tropaeum Traiani can be characterized as "Trajanic Monuments," thus implying that they were erected during that emperor's reign (AD 98–117), and therefore their clear stylistic differences cannot be accounted for by chronological reasons. Without archaeological evidence, including the inscription, and using stylistic criteria alone, the sculpture from the trophy might be considered later in date and an example of declining stylistic quality that some scholars see in late imperial art.

These are a few of the many drawbacks that must be considered in the establishment of stylistic sequences for artefacts and works of art. Once such a sequence has been established, new finds have to be integrated into it and placed in the correct chronological position on the basis of parallels and similarities to other objects of the same type already known, allowances being made for such things as the problems of geography, generations, and quality, as outlined above. The subjective factor comes into play here in judging parallels, and one may have to rely on the eye and judgment of the individual scholar to arrange objects in the correct order within the series.

Although the general rules of development for classical art and art-efacts are now generally accepted, agreement is not always universal, particularly when dealing with purely stylistic judgments without any clear chronological markers or obvious, dated parallels to help. The amount of stylistic change and the significance of any observed variations in a range of art objects of the same type may cause disagreement between scholars. The degree of movement, expressiveness, definition, and the overall treatment of a form are some of the qualities art historians use to arrange art into chronological sequences. The necessary judgments for making decisions in this area are based on training, experience, and often subjective feelings, and so can be controversial. Observable differences between works of art can be caused by circumstances other than time, as has been shown above in the case of Trajanic relief sculpture. In that case, however, the monuments were securely dated. Dating by style alone can be very difficult, particularly when dealing with some of the minor arts, which were mass-produced and often reflect many different influences. Factors such as preservation, technique, workshop practices, possible use of pattern books, or even workmens' individual initiatives or idiosyncrasies can be factors in any chronological judgments.[7]

In the ancient Greek and Roman world, stylistic sequences have been developed for numerous classes of objects by many scholars over the years. Once the objects can be arranged in succession based on changes in attributes, such as shape, decoration, method of manufacture, etc., one then has a relative sequence that shows the objects ranked before or after one another in the line of development. It will also show the relationships between objects within the line, and it may be possible to see how certain characteristics evolve and perhaps to understand the reasons for any changes. Since in a stylistic sequence some objects lie relatively near the beginning of the sequence, and others relatively near the end, the convention of using the relative terms "early" and "late" is used, with those lying stylistically between the two extremes characterized as "middle." It is important to understand that the terms "early," "middle," and "late" reflect no value judgments and are not synonymous with "crude," "developed," and "in decline." Thus an early Hellenistic figurine may show better workmanship than a middle Hellenistic one that is dated later. This example introduces the subject of dates, which is inherent in stylistic sequences. The sequence provides a relative date for an individual object and does not give a specific absolute date related to our own time. How absolute, numerical dates are arrived at and how they relate to stylistic, relative dating is outlined in Chapter 4.

Specific examples from the fields of architecture, sculpture, pottery, and the minor arts illustrate stylistic development in the Greek and Roman world.

The Doric Order is one of the three major orders of architecture developed by the Greeks within the tradition of post and lintel construction, which is basically a system of building that uses vertical uprights that support horizontal members. The three orders are the Doric, the Ionic, and the Corinthian, which vary from each other in proportion

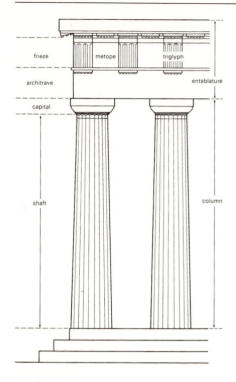

Figure 7   Corner of a building of the Doric Order. From Susan Woodford, *The Parthenon*, Cambridge, Cambridge University Press, 1981, fig. 2.14; drawn by Susan Bird

and architectural details, such as the shape of the capitals and the absence or presence of bases. The Romans adopted all three orders, often using them for decoration and scale, rather than as basic supports in the construction system. Variations and details of the orders have come down to today and are even used in contemporary architecture, in which some aspects of classical architecture, particularly in ornament, seem to be making a comeback.[8]

The Doric Order is illustrated in Figure 7 in its developed form. Two major characteristics set it apart from the Ionic and the Corinthian Orders. One is the triglyph and metope frieze composed of alternating vertically-grooved slabs (triglyphs – made up of two complete and two half grooves, the "glyphs") and flat, open spaces (metopes), which are sometimes decorated with sculpture or painting. The other diagnostic

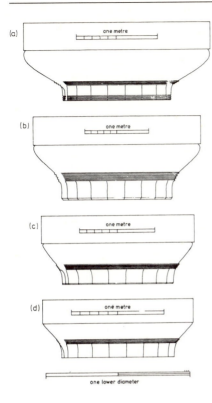

one lower diameter

Figure 8   Development of the Doric Capital. From J. J. Coulton, *Ancient Greek Architects at Work: Problems of Structure and Design*, p. 103, fig. 41. Copyright © 1977 by J. J. Coulton

characteristic of the Doric Order is the shape of the column, which is relatively short and squat compared to the Ionic and Corinthian columns. It is ornamented with twenty vertical channels or flutes separated by pointed ridges (Ionic columns have twenty-four flutes separated by flattened ridges), has no base (as do the Ionic and Corinthian columns), and is topped by a simple capital consisting of a swelling, cushion-like member, known as the echinus, topped by a rectangular slab, the abacus. The echinus serves as a transition from the vertical column to the horizontal upper portions of the entablature.

In the course of time, differences are observable in the shape of the forms employed to make up the Doric Order, and these cause a progressive change in the overall aspect of the building employing the order.

The general movement is away from heavy, squat proportions to slimmer and more elongated ones. A clear illustration of this can be seen in Figure 8, which shows how the profiles of Doric capitals developed in the space of about 200 years. What is significant is the change in shape of the bulging echinus and the proportions of the different elements of the capital to one another in these profiles that are scaled to one uniform lower diameter. The echinus, for example, is wide and spreading in the upper example from the Temple of Apollo at Corinth of about the middle of the sixth century BC. There is a definite angle where the curve of the echinus meets the lower surface of the abacus. At the Temple of Athena Alea at Tegea, approximately 200 years later, around the middle of the fourth century BC, the curve of the echinus has become more upright, and a sharper angle separates the echinus and the abacus. one of the fascinations with the study of Greek architecture is that within relatively rigid rules, such as those that apply to the shape and placement of the various parts of the orders, there is always change and development to be observed and accounted for. Modifications in detail often have chronological significance, and relative dates can be obtained by analysis of the change in the forms, such as the alteration in the configuration of the Doric capital. These broad transformations in the shape of the capital, as illustrated here, can generally provide dates only within about a half century, as long as the examples one is trying to fit into the scheme clearly belong to a single, obvious line of development, and there are no problems of geography, quality, material, etc., that might affect the evolution of the form. Dating on the basis of proportions is far from a precise method, must be used with caution, and even then yields only approximate dates. Differences in proportion between individual examples may result from other factors than date, and even capitals from a single building that were carved at the same time may differ in proportions, perhaps as a result of their placement, or variations intro-duced in the course of building by workmen, or even modifications established by the architect to fit his own sense of what was appropriate. There seems to have been no continuous, uniform evolution in the development of the Doric capital, but rather a number of major steps that can be seen in distinct groups of capitals that generally share similar proportions and yet are clearly different from one another; each capital in Figure 8 belongs to one of these groups. It is thought that this supports the idea that the Doric capital was designed using certain rules of proportion, and that specific changes in one or more of those rules are detectable in the differences in proportion that can be documented between the groups.[9]

Technical considerations can occasionally aid the dating of stone architecture and sculpture. Often different kinds of tools or alternate methods of working were used at distinctly different periods, and their traces on works in stone can be used to establish chronological indicators. An example of a change in technique in sculpture is the practice of indicating the pupil of the eye by a drilled hole, which is introduced in the reign of the Roman emperor Hadrian (AD 117–138). Prior to this technical innovation the eyeball in sculpture was simply painted. Such a specific change can be used for dating, but it must be recognize that a specific technical change might not be introduced everywhere at the same time, and, even when adopted, can often be used simultaneously with older techniques.

For sculpture, once again a general outline of stylistic development is understood, and there is a wealth of evidence in the form of actual sculptural works. However, the very existence of so much material, the long timespan involved when considering the whole of classical antiquity, its geographical distribution, and especially the relationship between Greek sculpture and Roman sculpture, make the subject an extremely complicated, if fascinating, one. Although a detailed discussion of Greek and Roman sculptural styles is beyond the scope of this book, a greatly simplified line of development within the single category of the standing male nude can be appreciated from Figures 9–14.[10]

At the beginning of the sixth century BC a series of nude, standing male figures was somewhat suddenly begun in Greek lands, and one of the earliest is illustrated in Figure 9. The statue, known as the "New York Kouros" after its present home in the Metropolitan Museum of Art in that city, originally came from Attica, from a site not far from Athens. These figures, known generically as *kouroi* (singular *kouros*, the Greek word for young man) are often rendered life-size or larger and were evidently used as dedications in sanctuaries, as funeral monuments, and even on occasion represented the gods. The New York Kouros stands squarely, facing forward, with abnormal proportions. The natural divisions of the body are indicated by bumps and grooves, reducing some anatomical details to pure pattern. The large, flat eyes, rendered without tear ducts and the schematic representation of the muscles and surfaces of the body are typical of this early stage of the representation of the human body in Greek sculpture. The stance, with the arms hanging straight down to the sides with the hands attached to the thighs by webs of stone, reproduces a common Egyptian pose. Most authorities therefore trace the general pose to Egypt, where similar statues had been produced for thousands of years. The Greeks, however, took this general form and,

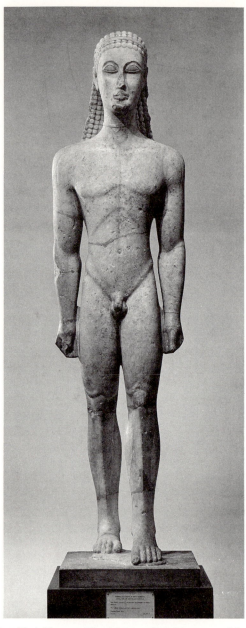

Figure 9   New York Kouros. The Metropolitan Museum of Art, Fletcher Fund, 1932 (32.11.1)

as they did with so many borrowings from the older civilizations of the Near East, quickly adapted it to their own uses. What is Greek is the nudity, unthinkable in any formal Egyptian context, the distribution of weight, evenly distributed rather than down the rear leg, and particularly the relatively crude rendering of the anatomy, which indicates the beginning stages of carving large-scale figures in hard stone.

In the course of the sixth century BC, a rapid change can be seen in the representation of the body, as is apparent from the statue in Figure 10, the Anavysos Kouros, dated to the third quarter of the century (i.e., about 550–525 BC) and also found outside Athens. A comparison of the two statues reveals that the later figure is less spare and exhibits more swelling forms than the earlier. Although the rigid, frontal pose is similar, with the one advanced leg and stiffly hanging arms (the break away from this stance is still in the future), the anatomy is no longer rendered in flat, sharply-defined planes, but more swelling, less patterned forms are used. The face too, shows these same changes with more volume and with rounded eyes taking the place of the flat, arched eye of the early example. It is clear that a development in shape has taken place, and the change to our eyes is one towards a more natural rendition of the forms of the human body, i.e., a development towards a more realistic depiction. The history of Greek sculpture from the sixth century through the Hellenistic Age can and has been discussed within the framework of this movement towards and sometimes even beyond (in some Hellenistic sculpture) the realistic rendering of forms observable in everyday life, whether of the human body or even of the drapery that sometimes clothes it. Whether this is correct for the whole period or not, as far as the intentions, perceptions, and abilities of the ancient Greeks is concerned, is seldom explored, for this type of approach allows modern scholars to set up usable stylistic sequences that are easily taught and perceived and that also train the eye. It seems obvious that the statue in Figure 10 is more developed in terms of the depiction of human anatomy than the *kouros* in Figure 9, and whatever the reasons for the change, it is clearly visible. After the sixth century, things become more difficult, and such a clear development is often not easily found.

Figure 11 illustrates one of the large bronze figures found in the sea off Riace, Italy in 1972. Two standing male figures were recovered, and their identity and origin are still debated. Most scholars, however, would date the statue in Figure 11, Riace A, *on stylistic grounds* to the middle of the fifth century BC or slightly earlier. The question of date is complicated in this case by our lack of much original full-scale comparative material in bronze for this era, the High Classical period of Polykleitos and

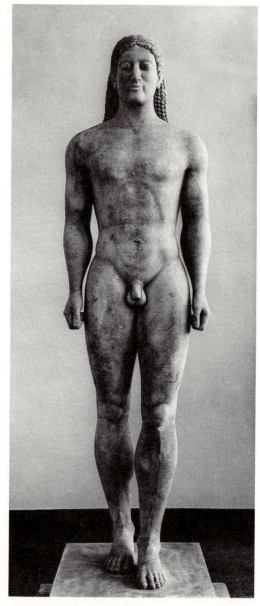

Figure 10   Anavysos Kouros. National Museum, Athens

Pheidias. Bronze is much too easy to melt down and reuse, and this is of course a problem that concerns all of antiquity, not just the fifth century BC. Accordingly, these major sculptors' works are known only indirectly through what are thought to be Roman copies and other even more indirect evidence, such as scanty literary references and small copies or adaptations of later times. Only a very few other life-size bronzes of the Classical period exist, and thus comparisons from what is known (always desirable and devoutly looked for by the art historian) are difficult at best. Several features of these new figures, especially the very modeled treatment of natural forms, is surprising and does not completely fit with what many scholars thought they knew of fifth-century BC style. A comparison of the anatomy and stance of this figure with the two previous ones indicates that again a change has occurred. The position is no longer the frontal stance of the kouros type, and the weight has now shifted to one leg, setting up a movement within the body not present in the earlier examples. This is emphasized by the head turned towards the supporting leg. Attributes have been added: for Riace A, a shield on his left arm (the internal shield strap is still preserved) and probably a spear in the right hand, both now missing, that may have helped to identify him, at least for the ancient viewer if not for us. The anatomy is massive in comparison with that of the Anavysos Kouros, and its swelling forms and the overall heroic impression of the figure shows clearly how far the sculptural style has developed in a relatively short span of time. The Riace figure, with its perfectly developed body, is seen by some writers as a representative of the idealizing tendency in the sculpture of the fifth century BC. The representation of the human body in an ideal form reached a peak of popularity in Athens in the third quarter of the fifth century, and this style of representation was very influential, reappearing throughout antiquity with greater or lesser influence on contemporary tastes in sculpture.

The nude, male form became a standard method of representing heroic figures, and the massive, bronze "Hellenistic Ruler" of the second century BC illustrates the model as used in the Hellenistic period to exalt a ruler (Figure 12). It may find the origin of its form in a portrait statue of Alexander the Great, whose general aspect, with one arm elevated and holding a lance, is preserved for us in a small Roman statuette. Which ruler the large Hellenistic bronze portrayed is debated, and although identifications have been made on the basis of coin portraits, no certainty has been attained. The over-life-size figure shows a mixture of stylistic traits, a common phenomenon in Hellenistic sculpture that adds to the difficulty often encountered in ordering Hellenistic art in a

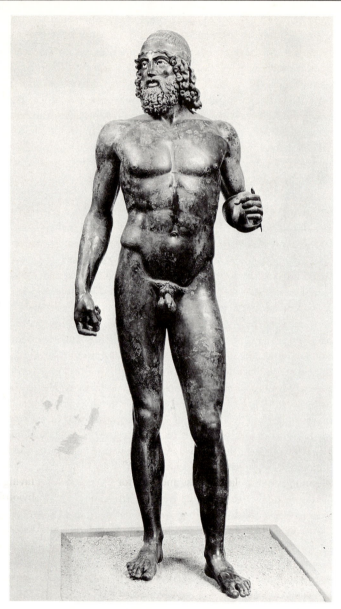

Figure 11   Riace Figure A. Reggio Calabria

reasonable chronological framework. The thick body with its projecting muscles and veins owes much to the classical tradition of the fifth century BC (compare Riace A, Figure 11), but goes beyond it in overall modeling. Also, the proportions, especially the small head and the position of the arms, are seen by some scholars as reflecting fourth-century styles. The head with its distinctive features and expression seems to be a portrait, and the general impression of the statue is that of a powerful ruler, conveyed as much by the stance as by the size and heroic nudity. These kinds of dramatic characteristics become important in the later periods of Greek art, and assessments of their appearance, force, and relative value are often part of the evidence used by art historians when establishing relative dates.

Hadrian's reign (AD 117–138) marked a period of revival and interest in Greek art, a phenomenon that occurs quite often in the history of art in the western world. This can appear in differing forms, varying from outright copies of Greek works to a full range of adaptations and interpretations that relate to a specific Greek style to a greater or lesser extent. An example of an interpretation of classical style is the statue of Hadrian's favorite Antinous, who drowned in the Nile in AD 130 (Figure 13). Here the pose is probably based on a classical prototype, and ideal nudity is once again employed, but the technique is Roman, even specifically Hadrianic. The musculature is softened and highly polished, which contrasts with the deeply cut hair and the individualized, if perhaps somewhat idealized, features. Untangling the different stylistic influences and quotations in a sculpture such as this Antinous can be complicated in this case by the fact that this particular statue was dedicated in Delphi, in Greece, and such a location in a famous Greek sanctuary could affect the style. Moreover, one might also have to consider the individual taste of the patron who commissioned the statue, in this case the emperor himself, and his particular interest and love for things Greek. Having a specific date for the death of Antinous from literary sources also obviously helps from a chronological point of view, but the unique nature of the circumstances that led to the creation of the images of Antinous must also be taken into account in any attempt to fit this statue into any general relative sequence of Roman sculpture.

The type of the heroized male nude continues throughout the Roman period and is illustrated by the over-life-size bronze in New York, thought by some to represent the soldier–emperor Trebonianus Gallus, who ruled briefly during the troubled third century AD (251–254) (Figure 14). Standing just under 8 feet in height (2.43 meters), the massive, ill-proportioned statue must have been intended to impress and overwhelm

Figure 12   Hellenistic Ruler. Museo Nazionale dell Terme, Rome

in a manner appropriate for a work that conveys imperial authority. A comparison with the Hellenistic Ruler (Figure 12) indicates how much change can occur over time within a specific type that originated in the Greek world and then was continued and developed by the Romans. Both figures show similarities in stance and position; both, for instance, are shown in heroic nudity and held lances, though in opposite hands. However, the Roman work with its static stance and odd proportions indicates a clearly different style than that of the Hellenistic work. Its differences from the earlier model on which it is largely based can of course be explained in a number of ways beyond that of the taste of a later time. Provincialism or even an incompetent artist may bear some responsibility for this statue, which appears artistically inferior to most modern observers within the context of third-century Roman art.

One final example of the continued life of Greek sculptural subjects and styles can be seen in Figures 15 and 16. A comparison of the two reliefs indicates that Figure 16, made about 100 BC, was clearly copied from the relief that is pictured in Figure 15, a slab from the parapet of the Nike Temple in Athens of about 420 BC, showing two Nikes, or Victories, leading a bull to sacrifice. A close examination of the two sculptures shows that the later one does not attempt to copy its model completely, as some think many Roman copies of famous Greek sculpture may have done, but alters the model in such fundamental ways that it represents a style in itself. This relief is one of a large number of reliefs and other sculptural works that were produced in the Late Hellenistic period and into imperial times that copied, with more or less adaptation, works of the Greek past. This adaptation of the Nike parapet frieze belongs to this tradition, and the style it represents has been called "Neo-Attic." The earliest workshops appear to have been set up in Athens, and the whole genre was apparently developed to feed the huge Roman art market that was hungry for Greek sculpture. In the examples here, it is sculpture of the late fifth century BC that has been adapted to form a more decorative presentation for contemporary Roman taste. The flat folds of the swirling drapery should be compared to the fifth-century BC original. Note that the wings of the Victories on the original relief have been omitted by the Neo-Attic sculptor, and the position of the Nike on the left has been changed so that her restraint of the lunging bull has been turned into an unstable, affected gesture. Later use of earlier stylistic details and even compositions, as here, is not an uncommon occurrence in the history of Greek and Roman sculpture and can usually be fairly easily identified by students familiar with the earlier periods whose art was adopted or adapted.

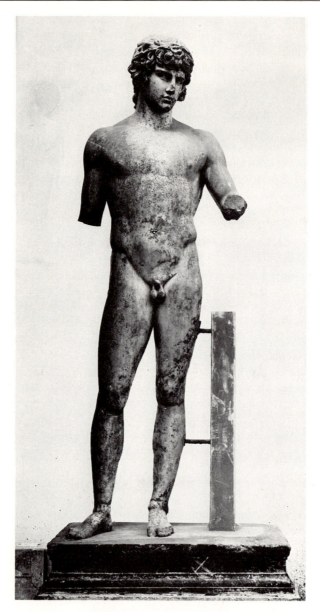

Figure 13   Antinous, Delphi

Figure 14   Trebonianus Gallus. The Metropolitan Museum of Art,
Rogers Fund, 1905 (05.30)

As has been demonstrated, relative chronology as applied to the sculpture of the Greeks and the Romans is a complicated undertaking, depending on analysis of stylistic change in the light of many varying factors, often including changes in detail. The few examples presented above indicate that in matters of style it is the eye of the scholar that has to make the determinations of relationships and produce a stylistic sequence. In a two-dimensional art such as painting, it is also often details as well as overall stylistic change that tell the story.[11]

A distinctive manner of decorating pottery was developed in the Greek city of Corinth in the seventh and sixth centuries BC. The decoration typically consists of rows of animals, both mythological and real, often arranged in symmetrical groupings, and this animal style is divided by scholars into two chronological phases – the Protocorinthian Style of the seventh century and the Corinthian Style, which evolves from it towards the end of that century. The rise and dissolution of this animal style has been documented by scholars, and two chronologically separate examples of it are illustrated in Figures 17 and 18. Figure 17 is a detail from one of the figured panels of a vase from the second half of the seventh century BC by a painter given the modern name of the Painter of Vatican 73, and the whole vase is shown on the left in Figure 19.[12] The detail shows two panthers looking out at the viewer, together with a slim sphinx who looks straight ahead. The figures are painted in the black-figure technique, a method invented at Corinth. In this technique figures are painted in solid, black silhouette on the light background of the clay body of the vase. Details are added by cutting thin lines down through the silhouette, into the surface of the vase, producing incised lines that are used for details and definition of musculature as well as the outlines of the figures, as can be seen in Figure 17. Added colors, usually purple and white, are used to enliven the black forms, but these are often worn away, leaving only a discoloration on the black where the added color has been applied. In the second half of the sixth century BC black-figure is superseded by red-figure, which in a sense is a reverse of the earlier technique, for the figures are red and the background is painted black. The figures are left, or reserved, in the reddish, clay color of the surface of the vase, and details are produced by thick, black lines in relief and also by diluted black in a variety of tones. Added colors are restricted to purple, at least at first, and the use of incision dies out.[13]

Figure 18 is a detail from another animal frieze, dating from approximately the first half of the following century, and it was painted by a painter known as the Ampersand Painter because of the distinctive way in which he depicts the tail of his sphinx.[14] Here two panthers frame that

Figure 15 Two Nikes and bull from the parapet of the Nike Temple on the Acropolis. Acropolis Museum, Athens

BACCANTI
CON TORO DIONISIACO

Figure 16 Neo-Attic adaptation of the relief in Figure 15, Uffizi, Florence

mythological creature. Although the two groups are composed basically of sphinxes and side-facing panthers and appear at first glance to be very similar, there are distinct differences between the paintings, some of which are the result of the individuality of each artist, such as the tail on the Ampersand Painter's sphinx and the way each artist handles the incision. However, other differences are more general and indicate stylistic development that has chronological significance. One of these changes can be seen in a comparison of the animals, which are more elongated in the later painting. This is a general tendency in Corinthian painting as time goes on and has been explained as a device to fill greater amounts of space more quickly as mass production of this popular pottery develops. Presumably fewer, longer animals take less time to paint than a larger number of shorter, more compact ones. Possibly also the extended wings of the sphinx are an indication of this stimulus. The filling ornaments also change, from a single, central dot connected by spokes to an outer circle of dots (the "dot rosette") of the seventh century to incised rosettes and simple blobs, which are easier and quicker to draw. A specialist, then, observing these differences can tell, even from a single fragment of a painted scene, approximately where it would fall chronologically within the general stylistic development of Corinthian painting.

Once a specific style has been recognized and its internal development understood, it is useful to be able to assign a length of time to it and if possible to each of its phases. Two problems are involved at this point. The first is judging when a particular style, for instance the Protocorinthian Style of Corinthian vase-painting of the seventh century BC, is sufficiently changed so that it can be designated as the succeeding Early Corinthian. The second problem is to decide how many years the Protocorinthian Style lasted before it took on the characteristics and hence changed into Early Corinthian. The first problem is a matter of definitions. An obvious example concerns filling ornaments; dot rosettes are characteristic of Protocorinthian and incised rosettes of Corinthian. These kinds of distinctions are, of course, not always so clear, and occasionally transitional styles are recognized that combine features of two other styles and act as a bridge between them. The olpe of the Painter of Vatican 73 (Figures 17 and 19) in fact belongs to the Transitional Style of Corinthian vase-painting, which comes chronologically between Protocorinthian and Early Corinthian.

Scholars use all available evidence to try and judge the length of time a particular style of painting existed. (This exercise has been called "stylometrics!") Number of examples is clearly an important criterion that might indicate the length of time a specific style of painting was

Figure 17   Detail of panthers and sphinx from Corinthian olpe by the Painter of Vatican 73, Museum of Art and Archaeology, University of Missouri, Columbia, Missouri

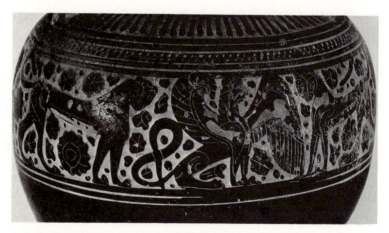

Figure 18   Detail of panthers and sphinx from a Corinthian pyxis by the Ampersand Painter, Greek, first quarter sixth century BC, *c.* 580 BC, 17.8 × 15 cm, Museum Purchase Fund, 1905.343. © 1990 The Art Institute of Chicago, All Rights Reserved.

produced. Historical evidence, archaeological evidence, such as comparisons with other schools of painting, comparative anthropological evidence, reasonable theories, and even guesswork can all be used. In the case of Corinthian painting styles, the time spans assigned for the development of the different stages are ultimately based on historical references, tied to archaeological evidence, and combined with some generalized speculation. See Chapter 4 for how the chronology of Corinthian pottery has been developed.

There is another problem, however, that the ancient art historian or archaeologist often has to face that does not arise in many later fields of art history, and that is the problem of preservation. The animals in both our examples are well enough preserved to be able to distinguish style, and even details. This is not usually the case, and archaeologists often have to try and date their strata on a handful of badly-preserved sherds, which in many cases do not come from decorated pottery but from the coarse household ware that is ubiquitous in excavations. Where fragments or sherds of painted, fine pottery do exist, their decoration may not only be almost completely destroyed but possibly not even diagnostic. It must be emphasized that the stylistic sequences that have been established for relative dating are only useful for the field archaeologist if a recognizable example of a given type shows up in the trenches in a significantly stratified context and in sufficient numbers. These problems of preservation and discovery of course also affect architecture and sculpture; fragments of sculpture are much more common in excavations than whole statues!

Often, dates can be derived from the observation of the typology of a particular pottery shape. Typology can be defined in this context as the study of changes that take place over time to the shapes of pots. These changes can affect the whole vase or its profile or its proportions, or even only small details, such as the contour of feet or handles. Once these changes are recognized and understood as far as their development is concerned, the shape of a handle or the curve of a body fragment can give a clue to the relative date of the object from which it came.[15]

Similarity of shape does not, however, guarantee similarity of date. Figure 19 shows the vase painted by the Painter of Vatican 73, whose animal frieze has been discussed above (p. 46), and a smaller version of the same shape. The smaller *olpe* (the technical name for this vase shape) dates later than the Corinthian example and was in fact made in Etruria by the Etruscans, who in the sixth century copied or adapted imported Corinthian pottery.[16] The Etruscan painter decorated his version of the Corinthian olpe with a different kind of animal style, employing only one band and much larger

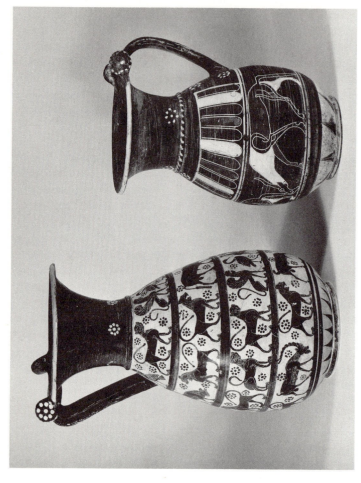

Figure 19 Protocorinthian and Etruscan olpai, Museum of Art and Archaeology, University of Missouri, Columbia, Missouri

animals painted in a different color scheme. The Etruscan grazing deer, although well drawn, are proportionally different and lack the crisp naturalism of their Corinthian model. The whole decorative scheme as applied to the pot and its technique is clearly not Corinthian. The Etruscan olpe belongs to the early years of the sixth century BC, the Corinthian one to the second half of the seventh. Thus, basically the same shape can be used in two different cultures in chronologically distinct periods.

However, good chronological sequences can be developed that show the development of vase shape when one particular category of pot can

Figure 20   Black-glazed kantharoi from the Athenian Agora

be traced over time within a single, well-known area with enough examples to provide a meaningful sample. Four black-glazed Attic drinking-cups, known as kantharoi, from the Athenian Agora are shown in Figure 20. They represent a particularly numerous category of vessels that were made in Athens and have been found in a number of well-dated contexts. Although they all share the same basic footed, two-handled shape, an obvious development towards taller and slimmer proportions can be seen, especially if one compares the examples at either end of the series. All four kantharoi belong to the fourth century BC, the earliest (on the left) dating to the second quarter of the century and the latest (the last two on the right) to about 300 BC, so a recognizable change at least in this particular shape can occur fairly rapidly. The four kantharoi illustrated here are in fact from the same closed deposit, and its date rests on archaeological evidence that combines datable artefacts with historical probability (see Chapter 5, p. 82). The dates assigned to the kantharoi have been developed in light of the closing date of the deposit and evidence from other datable deposits in the Agora and elsewhere.[17]

Shape change can also be traced in some objects of everyday use. Although most common instruments and implements do not change very much over time or have not been examined closely enough to recognize any such development, close study of some common objects can indicate developments in shape that can be set in believable sequences. An example of this type of study is illustrated in Figure 21, which shows profiles of loom-weights found in excavations in levels of the Greek period in the ancient city of Corinth.

Weaving in ancient times was undertaken on big looms which have not survived since they were made largely of wood. Numerous illustrations on black-figure and red-figure pottery and in wall-paintings, as well as ethnographic parallels, allow us to understand how these looms functioned. Ancient Greek looms belonged to the type known as the warp-waited vertical loom, in which the vertical or warp threads were held down and kept taut by heavy weights. These weights had different shapes in antiquity and could be pyramidal, round, or discoid and were made of clay, stone, or even lead. Those from Corinth in Figure 21 are conical in shape and made of clay.

Within the time represented by this series of profiles, from the late eighth to early seventh century of number I to the third and second centuries BC of XII–XIV, there is recognizable, if subtle, change in the curve of the sides of each weight, overall size and shape, and in proportions. Other considerations, such as material and finish, are not illustrated by the profiles, but were also taken into consideration in establishing the sequence. Such details as the development of beveling as seen in IV and V and its placement in respect to the overall curve of the side can be seen to be developmental features. Similarities of typology in two groups of profiles in this group of weights, I–III–VI and II–IV–V, suggest two separate lines of development even within this one category of common artefacts.

The arrangement of the clay loom-weights in a chronological sequence is based on their archaeological contexts from the excavations at Corinth, much in the same manner as the chronology of the kantharoi is based on evidence from the excavations in Athens and environs. There is unfortunately less historical evidence for Corinth than is available for Athens, although the date of 146 BC, the sack of Corinth by the Roman general Lucius Mummius, is often used as a known point for dating

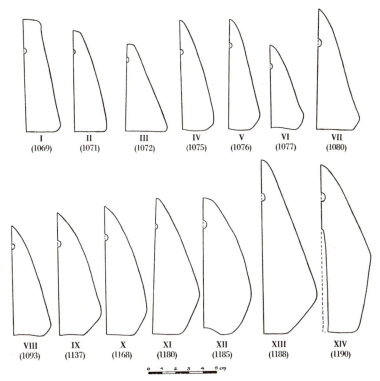

Figure 21   Profiles illustrating the development in shape of the Corinthian conical loom-weight. From *Corinth XII, The Minor Objects*, p. 149, fig. 23

in Corinthian archaeology. The absolute chronology of Corinthian loom-weights is expressed in more or less general terms, for no precision is possible with these common, locally-made objects that may have been in use for long periods. A general designation of within a half century or so for the popularity of a given shape is all that can be expected.[18]

Stylistic development or change can be seen in other classes of objects of everyday use as well, such as, for instance, the clay oil lamp (Figures 22–4) which can perhaps be classed as a "minor art," in comparison to the solid, plain loom-weight. Excavations in the Agora in ancient Athens have uncovered an uninterrupted sequence of lamps extending for more

Figure 22   Development of lamps from the Athenian Agora, 700–200 BC

than 1,000 years from the beginning of the seventh century BC to the sixth century AD and later. Terracotta lamps made for burning olive oil provided a common method of lighting in antiquity, and recognizable fragments of oil lamps are usually found in excavations. Lamps needed certain basic requirements, such as a container for the reserves of oil (which was usually the hollow body of the lamp itself), a handle of some type or some other provision for carrying, and a holder for the wick, which would allow one end to be immersed in the oil. A glance at the lamps in Figures 22–4 shows the variety in shape and decoration that existed over the years while still meeting the necessary three requirements. Within this sequence, there is also a technical progression of manufacture. The oldest lamps were handmade, followed by examples made on the wheel, and these were later superseded by those made in molds. These divisions are unfortunately only generally useful for chronology, for there was considerable overlap between the different methods of manufacture, with older methods still in use after a new procedure had been introduced into a region. There is, however, a definite progressive change in shape and decoration that is well illustrated when the examples can be seen laid out in sequence as in Figures 22–4. The oldest lamp, of the seventh century BC, is that at the upper left corner of Figure 22. It is handmade, with a completely open oil reservoir. This type is followed by wheel-made examples, with a progressive closing over of the oil container. By the Hellenistic period mold-made lamps become popular, and the space gained by closing over the oil reservoir begins to show some raised decoration. (See the bottom row of Figure 22 and the upper three rows of Figure 23.) Eventually, almost the whole oil reservoir is covered, leaving only a small filling hole, and the resultant disc area is often adorned with decorative designs or even figures and scenes (see Figures 23 and 24).[19]

Once a relative sequence has been developed and recognized, such as can be seen from the Athenian Agora, even fragments of similar lamps found elsewhere can be fitted into the sequence. Nozzle and handle shape, style and type of decoration, overall design, and methods of manufacture are all diagnostic features that can be recognized even on tiny fragments.

As has been illustrated above, it is possible, even without dates, to develop stylistic sequences for the different categories of art and artefacts in the Greek and Roman world. Providing a specific or absolute date for the objects is another matter. Various different types of evidence can be used, often together, to establish specific dates. Sometimes one object within a sequence can be dated by its archaeological association in datable contexts or with objects that are themselves datable. Often a single date or two within a stylistic sequence can serve to date, more or less, all the members of the sequence for they are then related stylistically (earlier or later) to the dated object or class. In other cases, a whole site,

Figure 23   Lamps from the Athenian Agora, 200 BC—AD 200

one part of it, or even one building can be associated with an historical event, perhaps a destruction from natural causes, war, or even from a known building program, thus providing at least a presumed date before

Figure 24   Lamps from the Athenian Agora, AD 200–700

which any objects found would have had to have been made. A single positive date within a sequence or for a site can be referred to as a "fixed" or "set point," and a chronological sequence can be draped over it like a rope hanging on a series of pegs on a wall. Remove one of the pegs and the rope will sag and change its position. Exactly the same thing will happen if an archaeological or historical set point is removed for one reason or another. The establishment of set points and their chronological significance is difficult at best, and involves interpretation of the archaeological record in relationship to the written record. The problems involved with interpreting the evidence are outlined in the following chapters.

Chapter 4

Absolute dating

Three categories of evidence can be used to determine a specific date for an object: historical, archaeological, and scientific. This chapter will explore these three categories.

A wealth of literary material is available from the Greek and Roman world, and a great deal about the ancient world can be learned and reconstructed from many different sources, ranging from the earliest literature of Greek times to the writings of the early church fathers. A general outline of the history of these ancient civilizations has been recovered from the ancient literature, especially the writings of Greek and Roman historians, by generations of modern historians, and the interpretation of texts continues to this day.

The historian of the ancient world works under several handicaps when it comes to attempting to record and understand the events and characters of that world. There is the major problem of the amount of evidence that is available for civilizations as far away from our own time as those of the Greeks and the Romans. For such remote periods information is uneven and seldom contemporary. Whereas historians dealing with other time-periods often have historical, or even biographical, sources that were written at the same time as the events they record, such a luxury is not common for the historian of the classical world. Texts are often incomplete or unclear, and the investigator is always operating with the handicap of the luck of preservation, since so much that was written in the literate Greek and Roman societies has completely perished. The written evidence that has survived must be carefully examined and its limitations understood. The historian has to be able to judge the relative value of a given writer from the point of view of that author as an historical source. This involves the nature of the work, its subject and scope, and the author's motive for writing it. Since the classical world saw the birth of the discipline of history, as we define it in the West, the modern historian also has to understand the historiography, the methods of historical scholarship, practiced by the ancient historians. The analysis of the relative value of a given ancient historian, his aims, principles, prejudices, and his reliance on earlier sources and their probable veracity, are all part of the task of the ancient historian and hence beyond the scope of this discussion.[1]

Although it has been said that "It is ... possible to construct a view of Roman civilization without recourse at all to archaeological evidence",[2] most historians, even of the relatively well-documented Roman Empire, commonly use evidence derived from archaeology to fill out and to confirm (or deny!) information derived from ancient literature. As for chronology, a general framework of more or less absolute dates has been worked out for the ancient Greek and Roman world that is based primarily on the literary evidence, supplemented and checked here and there by the archaeological record with such self-datable objects as inscriptions and coins. (See Chapter 1, pp.7–8, for the general chronological dates given to the various phases of the Greek and Roman civilizations.) The earlier one goes, the less reliable and the more fuzzy is the historical understanding of the periods and the absolute chronology.

The dates provided by ancient historians, or more accurately, the dates provided by modern historians' understanding of ancient historians, offer a framework into which the archaeologist must try to fit his or her material. The archaeological record provides relative chronology through stratigraphy and stylistic analysis, and the scholar turns to history to find an absolute chronology for the material. Often historical dates relate to major changes or catastrophes, which can be and often are used to provide a definite association for a destruction level or the filling of a well or the repair of a house. Here interpretation comes in, for there are dangers lurking in the ready acceptance of an absolute date derived from history. An excavator naturally wants to be able to interpret his remains in a way that relates to what we know, and historical dates have a seductive way of acting like magnets, attracting objects and remains to them. Historical events are, however, difficult to identify archaeologically, and there are very few recorded historical occurrences that are unambiguously recorded in the archaeological record. The destructions of Pompeii and Herculaneum in AD 79 are the exception. In these cities everything sealed by the destruction level must have been made prior to that specific year. In general, however, an accidental fire is difficult to distinguish from one that might be the result of enemy action, and few sites can be completely dug so that their physical history can be entirely recovered. Historical information also often refers to changes in social or political life, and that may be difficult to trace in the material record, although the attempt is often made. This is particularly true in areas that have a great amount of historical evidence associated with them, for instance the Agora of ancient Athens, where it seems that almost every feature is seen as containing evidence of some change that is recorded in the ancient sources.[3]

A danger in the use of literary evidence is the belief in the complete truth of a given source. For instance, a site stated to have been destroyed and presumably abandoned at a specific date is then not expected to yield any material subsequent to that date, and any evidence for later activity or occupation runs the risk of being suppressed or denied because it does not confirm the information provided by the written source.[4] Evidence may be interpreted or even unconsciously invented to agree with what the literature says. Conversely, the archaeologist can be in danger of preferring his interpretation of his own evidence when it appears to contradict a literary source and hence may declare that the particular source is "wrong". Obviously an analysis of any source must be part of the overall evaluation of all the evidence for a particular subject, and both the archaeologist and the historian must recognize that the fundamentally unorganized nature of reality often does not conform either with what an ancient author might have said or a later excavator found.[5]

Some of the most awe-inspiring phenomena for the ancient observer must have been the eclipses, especially the eclipse of the sun, which occurs when the sun, moon, and earth are in line, with the moon in the middle. Lunar eclipses, in which one sees the earth's shadow on the moon, are perhaps less dramatic, but none the less remarkable. Since celestial bodies in general obey laws of motion and gravitation, astronomers are able to calculate their positions in the past with a remarkable amount of precision. One author has estimated that the position of the moon in the sky 2 millennia ago can be calculated "with an error of less than 2°."[6] A number of reports of eclipses are known from ancient literature, and if specific dates can be attached to them, they can serve as historical fixed points. The most often cited of these is an apparent eclipse of the sun, reported by Herodotus and according to him predicted by the Greek philosopher and mathematician Thales of Miletus, that took place during a battle between the Lydians and the Medes.[7] The generally accepted astronomical date for this event is May 28, 585 BC. This date, however, has only historical significance and does not help in the dating of objects. Moreover, there are relatively few such specific references, and since eclipses are spectacular events, often associated with omens or supernatural events, they are often recorded by writers other than astronomers, leading to questions as to the correctness of the observations.[8]

A specific example of dates derived from literary sources that are used for establishing chronology are the founding dates for the Greek colonies established in Sicily and south Italy. The historian Thucydides, in his discussion of the background to Athens' doomed military expedition to Sicily, recounts the history of the Greek colonization of the area.[9] In the course of this, he gives the founding date of many of the colonies by relating them one to another. He states that one, Megara Hyblaea, was destroyed by the tyrant of Syracuse, Gelon, 245 years after it was founded. Much of the chronology of Gelon's career is known from several other historical references, and the date of his destruction of Megara can be determined to within a year or so, thus establishing its founding date. Once the date of the establishment of Megara is determined, that for Selinus can also be found, for the historian indicates that city was founded 100 years after Megara. More or less specific dates can thus be determined by this kind of calculation from Thucydides and other sources for the foundation of most of the western Greek colonies. Once a specific date is determined for a city and excavations are begun there, it is generally assumed that the earliest Greek pottery found in abundance is likely to belong to the colony's earliest years. This pottery is usually from the mainland city of Corinth, whose fine, painted wares were widely exported in the seventh and early sixth centuries BC and belong to the styles known as Protocorinthian and Corinthian, as has been discussed in Chapter 3 (pp. 46, 49–53). As a result of several generations of scholarship, the foundation dates of the colonies have been used as fixed absolute chronological points in the development of these pottery styles.

The tying in of absolute dates to a stylistic sequence of fine Corinthian pottery is relatively important, for this pottery, with its wide distribution in early Greece, provides evidence for the chronology of other types of material. For instance, a datable sherd in the construction fill of a building can provide a clue to that building's date of construction and perhaps to sculpture associated with it, and this in turn could be related to other sculpture or other arts. The chronology of Protocorinthian and Corinthian painting remains one of the firmest absolute chronologies for the early period of Greek art, but that is not to say that it has not been challenged in part as well as in its entirety in the past and even recently, based partly on a lack of confidence for most dates provided by ancient historians for the earlier periods of Greek civilization. Finds of Corinthian pottery considerably earlier stylistically than the accepted Thucydidean date for a particular colony's foundation have caused doubts and occasioned re-evaluation of the assumption that the earliest pottery found indicates the earliest settlers. Foreign pottery from graves might indicate imports, rather than the belongings of colonists, and it is always possible that unless a whole site can be excavated, which is an unlikely proposition, there might be areas of the earliest settlement that have not been discovered. On the other hand, if the important areas of the city, such as the religious and political centers, are located and fully excavated to their lowest levels, one can probably be relatively certain that the earliest material has been found. Once again, it is the context and the interpretation of the finds that is crucial.[10]

There is little direct evidence from ancient literature as to chronology for art. The ancients were poor art historians in our modern sense, but architects such as Vitruvius of the first century BC, encyclopedists such as Pliny the Elder of the first century, or travelers such as Pausanias of the second century, provide evidence that is priceless, though often difficult, obscure, or contradictory.[11]

Archaeological evidence for the dating of objects is usually relative, as has been outlined above, with stratigraphy often providing the clues for chronology. A few archaeological artefacts can be described as "self-dating," and can provide a specific chronological fixed point for other objects, features, or buildings, provided they are found in a reliable relationship to them. These objects relate to individuals or specific events whose dates are either known historically or can be determined.

Inscriptions, texts, or words written on or in some permanent surface, provide one of our major sources of knowledge of the classical world. They are a characteristic feature of that world and found in staggering numbers not only in the major cities of that civilization but throughout the whole extent of the ancient world wherever Greco-Roman civilization spread its influence. The discovery of an inscribed stone in a remote spot can even provide evidence for a hitherto unsuspected settlement, providing that the inscription had not been moved in later times far from its place of origin. Ranging from governmental decrees and official documents of various types through records of everyday life, such as military diplomas or market price-lists, to religious dedications and funerary inscriptions, they provide us with a great deal of information written in the actual words of the ancients themselves.

Unfortunately not all inscriptions clearly date themselves; many texts are fragmentary or include no obvious chronological information. These have to be dated with reference to both history and archaeology. Various criteria can be employed for assigning a date. For instance, historical evidence can be used to provide at least a general date. Political and historical events provide the opportunity for documentation, and social changes, such as new laws, can also affect the form or content of a given inscription. If the dates of such events or changes are known, even fragmentary texts can be related to them and can thus be assigned a date. Sometimes an inscription can be directly associated with other specific, documented objects or constructions. An inscription built into a later, dated monument, such as a fortification wall, obviously was carved before the wall was built; one found in an excavation in a sealed deposit can be at least relatively dated by the latest contents of that deposit. References in an inscribed text may refer, even indirectly, to individuals or occurrences that are independently dated, and the date of the inscription can then be worked out from these hints. Certain types of inscriptions are specific to particular periods or locations; one would not expect, for instance, to find a dedication to Asklepios in Athens before the end of the fifth century BC when the god's cult was first introduced into the city. To a lesser extent, the style of lettering and the forms of the letters in an inscription can have chronological significance. Letter forms and methods of writing change over time like everything else, and these can often provide at least an approximate date. Unfortunately, the relative dating of inscriptions on the basis of style is a difficult process as far as absolute chronology is concerned.

Many inscriptions do date themselves by their text, however, often by the inclusion of the name of a known ruler or magistrate or by a clear reference to a political or historical occasion whose chronology is known. This is particularly true in the case of documents written during the Roman Empire that include the name of a particular emperor, for the chronology of the rulers of the Empire is known. Hence, large Roman buildings often bore a dedicatory inscription lauding the emperor during whose reign they were erected, and even bricks in a public building often bear a stamp, which is a form of inscription, that will also give an emperor's name. A dated inscription can date a building and from that a whole complex of buildings, or perhaps provide a welcome fixed point for sculpture or other objects when it appears in association with them, as on some funeral monuments.

Other inscriptions date themselves by other systems that were also in use in the ancient world, as has been noted in Chapter 2 in the discussion of the various methods of recording time. Regnal years of the Hellenistic kings of Egypt is the method used to date a small number of pots used to hold human ashes in the cemeteries of Alexandria in the Hellenistic period. The name of the deceased as well as a numbered regnal year were painted or incised on many of these "Hadra Hydriae," so-named after a suburb in Alexandria where many were found in the nineteenth century AD. From these inscriptions the identification of the kings can be adduced, and since the dates of the reigns of the Hellenistic kings of Egypt are known, these inscriptions provide a fixed point not only for the development of shape and decoration of this particular type of pottery in the Hellenistic period, but also for the style and character of writing for the period and for any other artefacts that might be associated with the pots.[12]

Another method of dating, by era, is used by a funerary inscription already referred to in Chapter 2. In that case the inscription gives a specific year in the Seleucid era, which can be converted to AD 97/98 in our own calendar. This provides a fixed chronological point for the development of north Syrian funerary sculpture in the first century AD (see above, p. 13).

The value of inscriptions to chronology is self-evident, but unfortunately relatively few texts include such clear dates as can be found in the last two examples. Dated inscriptions are more common in the later periods, and their study by numbers of scholars has led to the establishment of chronological sequences of magistrates and rulers for many cities. The study of inscriptions is known as epigraphy.[13]

Coins are the most well-known type of self-dating find, and the study of coinage is known as numismatics.[14] A coin is defined as a piece of metal of a specific weight that is issued by some authority that guarantees its weight and purity. Starting with the earliest issues, coins bore designs and devices of the issuing authority as guarantee marks, called "types." It is not always clear to us what authority is referred to with some of the types on the earliest coins, but later certain designs become clearly associated with individual cities, such as the head of the goddess Athena for Athens. It was not until towards the end of the fifth century BC that the head of a living ruler, the Persian satrap Tissaphernes, first appeared on coinage at the Ionian city of Miletus. This practice did not become normal until the Macedonians, and their successors began regularly to identify coinage by the head of the monarch that issued it. Apart from some instances of posthumous issues, coins with portrait heads of rulers were issued during the reigns of those rulers. If that span of years is known, the coin can be dated. In the case of the coins of the Roman emperors, some are dated to the year, even to specific months, by their legends that include honors or titles whose dates of conferral are known. Unfortunately, relatively few coins are dated in this manner, and the great bulk of coins, especially of the earlier periods, do not carry specific dates. A coin's date must be determined with the same general combination of archaeological and historical evidence that is used for dating any find, such as inscriptions. There are, however, qualities unique to coins that can be used to help determine chronology.

Except for some of the early Roman Republican coins that were cast, coins are produced by striking. In this process a blank of metal is positioned over an engraved design (a die) cut into the surface of an anvil or other stable flat surface. A second die is positioned above the blank and then struck by a hammer, forcing the die into the surface of the blank and at the same time driving the under surface of the blank into the lower die. In this way two designs in relief are produced on both sides of the coin. Each die was separately made and wore out at different rates. The lower die, which formed the obverse of the coin, tended to last longer than that for the reverse, which was used like a punch and subsequently received more wear. Often the same obverse die is used with two or three reverse dies. The examination of die wear and the relationship of dies to one another in a series (die links) can yield relative dates for coins within the life of a single mint, which might itself be dated on historical grounds. Other methods of dating coins include analysis of wear that can indicate length of time in circulation, and study of the types portrayed from an art historical point of view.

Another method for determining chronology that is unique for coinage is the study of overstrikes and countermarks. Occasionally, instead of melting down coins or preparing new blanks, old coins are simply struck again, new types being superimposed over the old designs. The new coin is by definition later than the coin which is overstruck, and if traces of the earlier coin can be identified, a step towards a relative chronology can then be taken. This works particularly well if a dated issue from one city is overstruck by an undated issue from a second city. Countermarks can be seen as a cheaper and easier method than overstriking. The marks, usually punched into the coin, are generally small and do not obliterate the designs. The authority who countermarked the coins did it for various reasons; to revalue it, to guarantee its weight and content in the case of a foreign coin adapted for use elsewhere, or to mark a special occasion of issue. Overstrikes and countermarks may provide dates, if the historical events that caused them are identified; they can also be useful in providing information about the length of time coins were in circulation, as well as interesting evidence of monetary policy and mint practice.

Evidence from hoards, which are groups of coins deliberately buried together, can also often be used to determine chronology. Hoard evidence is difficult to evaluate, however, especially if the nature of the hoard is not apparent. A hoard of coins intentionally saved by an individual may be significantly different in make-up, having older coins and those of higher denomination, than a hoard composed of coins taken out of circulation at a time of danger. The nature of the hoard and, if possible, the reasons for its deposit must be evaluated, and this often depends on being certain that the entire hoard has been recovered, which can only happen in a controlled excavation. As in the analysis of any closed deposit, the date of the latest object provides the date of the closing of the deposit, and thus relative sequences can be established based on wear and other factors within the hoard itself. Much of the chronology of ancient coins has been established by the use of evidence from hoards.

Other objects than coins can make up a hoard. If datable coins are also included, they give a specific time after which the hoard must have been deposited, thus providing a fixed point for the manufacture of everything else in the closed deposit. Evidence for the stylistic and technical development of jewelry and gem-cutting in Roman Britain will, for instance, be greatly increased by the evidence recovered from a hoard found in England in 1985. The Snettisham hoard, found in Norfolk, was made up of material evidently from a jeweler's workshop and contained silver jewelry (including eighty-nine rings, as well as bracelets, chains, and pendants), silver scrap, ingots, engraved carnelian gem stones, and over 100 coins, the latest dating to AD 155. Thanks to the numismatic evidence and to the fact that the find was well-investigated and certain to be complete, the final study of this hoard will provide significant information for the functioning and products of a provincial jewelry workshop of the second century.[15]

It is, however, the circumstances of the find of any particular coin that determines its usefulness for dating anything, even if the coin itself is securely dated. A single coin can turn up almost anywhere, as has been indicated in the discussion of stratigraphy (p. 19), and unless from a well-sealed deposit or stratum, a single coin may be suspect. Given their potential importance to chronology, it is a pity that many coins found in excavations are often either too worn or too corroded to be legible. This seems to happen frequently with coins from important and significant contexts, much to the frustration and disgust of the excavator. Even worn or corroded examples can, nevertheless, have evidential value and may provide information on such topics as trade, or on particular circumstances in the economic, historical, or political spheres.[16]

Less well known, but of great use to the archaeologist, is the fact that for something in excess of 1,000 years transport amphoras carried impressed stamps on their handles. These large pots have already been cited as examples of differences in shape that do not primarily have chronological significance (Chapter 3, p. 26, and Figure 4, p. 27). Not only did their distinctive shapes announce their origins, but also the stamps, pressed into the wet clay of the upper surface of the handles before firing, often bore a device that was the emblem of the city from which the amphora came. These symbols, such as the rose, associated with the city of Rhodes, are often also found on coins of cities and serve there to identify the city as the particular authority guaranteeing the weight of the coin and the purity of its metal. Many amphoras also have their handles stamped with the name of an annually-appointed official or magistrate. The stamp usually reads something like "in the period of office of so-and-so," and this is probably a control or tax mark, or perhaps even a vintage date in the case of amphoras that carried fine wine. If the individual can be identified and the date of his period in office determined, an absolute date can be given to the amphora. Sequences of dated stamps have been established for a number of types of amphoras, and research continues in this rewarding field. Figure 25 illustrates a rectangular dated stamp on the handle of a Rhodian amphora. Here the name of the official, "Ariston," is given, preceded by the word "epi," forming the formula for the period in office. This formula takes two lines, the last three letters of Ariston's name forming the second line. The bottom line of the stamp contains the name of a Rhodian month, "Sminthios." This stamp can be dated to the years between 182 and 176 BC from finds of other stamps bearing this name in dated contexts and from other evidence derived from the study of the sequences of names of dating officials and the calendar in use in Rhodes in the Hellenistic period.[17]

Inscriptions, coins, and amphora stamps are three classes of material that are relatively abundant and that provide absolute dates for themselves in one way or another. In addition to these, there are a few other types of artefacts that may also give absolute dates, but practically all have problems associated with their interpretation as far as chronology is concerned, and most of them only provide dates for other objects if they are clearly associated with them in some way.

Many Greek vases from Athens of the Archaic and Classical periods, roughly from the third quarter of the sixth to the third quarter of the fifth century BC, have written inscriptions as part of their figured scenes. Many of these are men's names in the formula "so-and-so kalos" and are thus called "kalos names." The word "kalos" has a range of meanings

Figure 25   Stamped amphora handle, scale 1:1. Museum of Art and Archaeology, University of Missouri, Columbia, Missouri

in Greek including "beautiful" or "comely," and although the exact meaning of the term is debated, it has generally been thought that the youths named as kalos were aristocratic favorites of the day in the wealthy Athenian society that would be the main market for these highly-decorated vases. Some 300 names are known, and it would seem reasonable that in a relatively small society such as Athens of this period, some at least of the individuals named as "kalos" in their youth might appear later as mature men in the historical record. If a particular person named as kalos on a vase could be identified with a later, dated, historical figure, then counting back to the period when the individual might be considered kalos would theoretically give a date for the vase. There are, however, only a few individuals about whom enough is known to allow this kind of computation, and there can be terrible confusion over identifications, given the ancient Greeks' habit of naming their sons after their grandfathers and other relatives, thus providing for frequent repetition of names within a family. Furthermore, the rules governing the use of the term kalos are uncertain, particularly at what age and for how long a youth could be so described. Estimates of the length of time a youth could be considered kalos have ranged from the mid-teens, to even as late as 25. In general, the use of kalos names to determine chronology is considered too full of problems to be of much use, other than indicating relative chronology. For instance, if two vases painted by different painters both bear the same kalos names, they are likely to be more or less of the same date.[18]

A slightly different problem of identification confronts attempts to date ostraca, fragments of pottery on which were inscribed the names of prominent Athenians who were candidates for ostracisms held in the city during the fifth century BC. The institution of ostracism was a feature of Athenian democracy that was intended to allow the citizens to banish an individual whom they thought might be planning to seize the government and set himself up as a tyrant. It was in use for a relatively short period, about seventy years, and then was abandoned, for it quickly became a political tool for defeating an opponent. When a vote was taken for an ostracism, the citizens inscribed on their ostraca the names of the individuals they would like to see banished from the city. Occasionally, at least some of these were prepared ahead of time, indicating organized campaigns against certain individuals, for a number naming one individual have been found written in the same hand. A great many of these ostraca have been found in excavations in Athens, and the names of numerous famous politicians of the time are inscribed on them. The historical sources record a number of individual ostracisms during the period in which this practice was in use, but one cannot be certain in which ostracism a particular ostracon might have been used, for there may have been some votes that were not recorded, and a particularly active politician could be named at any number of times. Although in most cases the identification of the individual is assured, since the ostraca usually give the full name, still the connection with a specific dated ostracism is unclear; the use of ostraca for a precise chronological determination is, therefore, marginal.[19]

Another type of object bearing names that might be identified and thus provide chronological evidence is lead sling bullets. Cast in terracotta molds, these small, almond-shaped missiles often have raised decorations consisting of symbols, hortatory remarks (such as "take this" or "eat this!"), or names expressed in the possessive form. In the ruins of the northern Greek city of Olynthus, for instance, a number of bullets were found with the inscription "of Philip," and our sources tell us that the city was destroyed by Philip II, Alexander the Great's father, in 348 BC. Only a relatively few bullets were apparently adorned with the names of major historical personages, such as Philip or Alexander, and most have the names of generals or of unit commanders who were probably in charge of the slingers using the missiles. The problems associated with the identification on vases and ostraca of ancient names also apply to these names, although the possibilities are restricted to military commanders. Even if an identification can be made, there is no certainty that the right individual has been found, and the overall chronological importance of even an identified bullet is minimal unless it is found in a significant context, such as the destruction level at Olynthus. No stylistic development in sling bullets has so far been documented, for the shape does not seem to have changed over time to any great extent.[20]

Finally, some spectacular individual finds are self-dated and illuminate history but have had little effect on the chronology of classical archaeology. A badly-preserved round, bronze shield found in the excavations in the Athenian Agora at the bottom of a cistern bears an inscription in punched-out letters across its convex surface: "The Athenians [dedicated this] from the Lakedaimonians at Pylos." One of the great victories of Athens in the Peloponnesian War was the defeat of a Spartan detachment at the island of Sphacteria in the area of Pylos in the western Peloponnese in 425/4 BC. Thucydides relates that 292 Spartans were captured and interned in Athens. Apparently their shields were dedicated in a building in the Agora, the Stoa Poikile (called "the Painted (Poikile) Stoa" from the paintings that adorned it), and were still there in the second century AD, for the traveler Pausanias records them, together with other trophies. The Agora shield, whose inscription is consistent in its letter forms for a fifth-century date, must be one of the captured shields from the battle, which for some reason, unknown to us, was separated from the others and found its way into the cistern. The shield itself is then dated to a specific year and could conceivably be used as a fixed point in the development of shields, but such a development has not been recognized in sufficient chronological detail to make the Pylos shield significant, nor was its context chronologically important, since it was found in a cistern that was closed in the third century BC.[21]

The objects that have been designated here as self-dating are generally more abundant and more reliable in the later periods, the coinage of the Roman Empire being the best example, because an individual coin can in many cases be dated to a very short span of years. As has been indicated, the major problem with this sort of evidence rests on its find spot and its relationship with whatever needs to be dated from it. Coins, for instance, are notorious for being illegible or appearing in the wrong places in excavations, i.e., mixed fills or dumps where they are not chronologically significant. The category of "worthy things from unworthy places" is well known to any field archaeologist. A single object, especially a small one, can travel, and even if a datable object is found in a closed deposit, it is important to understand that it in fact only indicates a time after which the deposit was formed, as explained in the discussion of stratigraphy in Chapter 3 (pp. 18–23, 25). In other words, the sealed deposit could not have been closed before the object was produced, but could have been closed any time after it was made.

Datable objects found in useful archaeological contexts can be used with caution to provide chronological fixed points. For instance, a datable coin found clearly sealed in an uncontaminated level under a later floor provides at least one absolute date and can be used as part of the evidence to establish, with some probability, a whole relative building sequence for a building complex.[22] Thus, the interpretation of the archaeological context of a dated object is the crucial point.

Attempts to determine absolute dates through scientific means have been one of the major developments in archaeology in the last fifty years.[23] New discoveries in the scientific sphere have been followed eagerly by the archaeological community, and a number of different methods and procedures tried out. Classical archaeology has been slow, some might say backward, in investigating scientific methods of absolute dating, for the wide range of deviation in absolute dates derived from most of the techniques precludes their usefulness. Most of the traditional methods of dating in historic cultures can produce more precise calendar dates. Scientific dating methods are applicable and heavily used in prehistoric archaeology, where specific dates cannot be attained with precision, and a relatively long span of years is acceptable. There are, however, three methods of scientific dating that have been used for classical archaeology with varying success.

The most commonly used absolute dating system is radiocarbon dating, which depends on the decay over time of carbon-14, a radioactive isotope of carbon that exists in every living thing and begins to decay after the organism dies. Measurement of the remains of carbon-14 in ancient wood or charcoal, for instance, can provide a date when the wood ceased to live. The method is complex, needs a large number of samples for any precision, and is affected by a number of variables involving the rate of production of the isotope in nature over the centuries. Moreover, timbers in wooden constructions can be reused for a great many years after they were cut, and problems of the variability of samples and of contamination further complicate the usefulness of this method. In addition, a number of adjustments keep being made in the radiocarbon time-scale to the point that some loss of confidence might be expected from the archaeological community.

Dates derived from carbon-14 research are expressed with a standard deviation of plus or minus a number of years, often as much as several centuries. As mentioned above, traditional methods of dating historic cultures, such as those of the Greeks and the Romans, are usually more precise. In fact, carbon-14 is often tested against known historical events, which have been dated to within a few years from historical sources. The most recent adjustments of the carbon-14 chronologies have been undertaken by calibrating them against dates provided by dendrochronology, which in many places can provide specific dates with a higher level of certainty.[24] For a specific example of the use of the carbon-14 method to attempt to date a single event in the first century AD at Cadbury Castle in Britain, see p. 78.

Dendrochronology is based on the observation that yearly tree growth is recorded by the rings observable in a cross-section of a tree trunk. Thus, theoretically, a tree can be dated to the year it was felled, providing (ideally) a section from bark to the center can be observed. Sequences developed for trees of one species in specific areas are often linked to historical dates determined from external sources. This is particularly true in the American West, where a tree sequence based on the bristlecone pine extends back over 8,500 years before the present. A similar sequence based on the western European oak is reported to stretch back over 9,000 years, and it has been used, for instance, to date a Roman bridge at Trier, whose beams came from trees that were calculated to have been cut down in AD 119.[25]

Such specific dates promise great advances for chronology, and dendrochronology has already been used for calibrating and checking the precision of carbon-14 dates, as mentioned above. However, as in most scientific dating techniques, there are problems, particularly in regard to the technique's use for classical archaeology in the Mediterranean area. Not all trees are sensitive to environmental conditions, and even in those that are, well-preserved samples are needed, and these are not often available within an archaeological context. At best, dendrochronology can tell only when a tree was cut down, and later use, reuse, and such other variables as, for instance, a possible timber trade, must also be considered. The problem of reuse is of course also acute for the process of dating by carbon-14.

Although great strides have been made in developing various tree-ring sequences from the classical world, these are not tied to specific dates, and are thus referred to as "floating." No absolute Mediterranean tree-ring chronology has yet been established.[26]

Thermoluminescence dating is based on the fact that clay and a few other inorganic materials absorb small amounts of nuclear energy from natural radiation. The procedure, in relation to clay, involves measuring the amount of radiation absorbed by a ceramic since it was last fired. If a fired clay object is heated to about 380° centigrade, the stored energy is released, producing light, which, when measured, can indicate the total dose of radiation that has been absorbed by the object since its radioactivity was last released by firing.

The deviation from the actual date of a single sample is in the 7 to 10 per cent range, which on a single sample from the first century AD could be approximately 130 years. The range of years involved with this technique is considered too great to be useful in classical archaeology, although much better precision has been reported for some pottery from Romano-British sites. Thermoluminescence dating is perhaps most commonly used for the authentication of ancient pottery, where extreme precision is not necessary, the goal being to determine if the particular object is ancient or was fired in later times.[27]

The different means of determining absolute dates outlined above are most often employed in combination, depending on the individual site and the kinds of evidence available. An example of this use of various methods comes from the excavations at Cadbury Castle, an Iron Age hillfort located in Somerset in southern England.[28] Here, digging in 1970 uncovered the south-west entrance of the fortified town, consisting of a narrow, stone-lined passage, with a guard-chamber to one side. In this passage-way was found evidence of a massacre, consisting of dismembered human skeletons of some thirty men, women, and children, iron weapons, and over 100 bronze brooches, used in ancient times for fastening clothing. The obvious interpretation was that this was the aftermath of a battle at the gates of the town and that those killed in the battle had been left unburied and their bodies probably torn apart by wild animals. Subsequently, the fortifications were intentionally demolished, probably by a detachment of Roman soldiers, the remains of whose camp, field oven, and discarded pieces of recognizably Roman armor were found elsewhere on the site. How could this dramatic event, illustrated so vividly in the archaeological remains, be set securely in history? In fact, several categories of chronological evidence existed to provide an explanation and a date for this occurrence.

Stratigraphy clearly indicated that the gate's fortifications belonged to the Late Iron Age and had undergone strengthening just prior to the massacre. Historical sources provide the context for such a conflict with accounts of the Roman invasion in AD 43 and the continued campaign to pacify the countryside through the defeat of the Boudiccan revolt in AD 60, an overall range of dates that broadly fits the archaeological evidence. The Latin biographer Suetonius records that the general Vespasian, later to become emperor, was in charge of one wing of the Roman advance into England after AD 43 and destroyed more than twenty towns in this general area. This would then seem a likely date for the massacre at Cadbury, especially since evidence of fighting and violent destructions was also known at other hillforts in southern England with Roman material clearly in evidence. At Maiden Castle some thirty-four skeletons were found intentionally buried in what the excavator called a "war cemetery." Many of the skeletons showed wounds consistent with those received in a battle; one had a Roman iron projectile point, perhaps from a small catapult, embedded in his spinal column and a portion of his right jawbone sliced away, presumably by a sword cut.[29] Thus, from the historical sources and parallel archaeological evidence, a date at the beginning of the Roman conquest, about AD 45, would be appropriate.

However, as often happens, the archaeological evidence was difficult to reconcile with this early a date. The large numbers of brooches found at the massacre site could be fitted into a relative chronology for these types of objects, but some of them had previously appeared only in contexts later than that suggested at Cadbury, and the whole stylistic sequence was not well enough dated to provide a definite chronology for the development of the various types. Other finds such as the military weapons, four coins (latest, apparently unworn, dating from the reign of the Emperor Claudius, AD 42–54), local pottery, and other metalwork also did not provide a definite chronological point but could be appropriate for the AD 45 date. The remaining class of finds was the imported red Roman pottery, known as "Samian Ware" in Britain and *Terra Sigillata* elsewhere. This type of pottery was made in Gaul and can be dated with better precision than the other objects. Most of the Samian Ware from Cadbury apparently belonged to the reign of Nero (AD 54–68) and that from the Roman camp-site "not earlier than the 70s," while "early Roman" wares were also detected in the level with the brooches and the bodies.[30] If the camp-site was in fact for a working party to demolish the walls, then it is unlikely that it would have occurred some thirty years after the battle. The suggestion was therefore made that Cadbury must have been by-passed in the initial invasion and that the destruction and massacre took place in the 70s. An historical reason for such a disaster, however, is difficult to find for so late a date, as the excavator himself realized.[31]

Further study convinced the excavator that the undecorated Samian pottery found at the camp-site could allow a date some ten years earlier, which would be more comfortable as far as the historical evidence is concerned.[32] The massacre could then be seen as an incident in the west connected with Queen Boudicca's revolt, and the date could then be as late as about AD 60 or 61.

The nature of the excavation, a destruction level with large amounts of burned wood, was ideal for the employment of the carbon-14 technique in an attempt to obtain a date. A number of samples was taken from the roof structure of the guard-chamber, the threshold of the Iron Age gate, and elsewhere and sent to a number of laboratories. A total of five readings was taken on each sample by different methods, giving some fifty individual carbon-14 values that represent spans of time. The results were, however, disappointing, with the range of dates too wide to be able to obtain a single, precise designation. Even when the most accurate results were considered, the carbon-14 procedure could only indicate that the event had taken place sometime during the first three centuries AD. Thus, for a single historical event the carbon-14 method only produces approximate dates within a range of some 200 to 300 years.[33] As we have seen, in this case traditional methods of archaeological interpretation linked with historical information were much more accurate, and this is true in most of the periods with which classical archaeology is concerned.

The dates of the massacre and destruction of the Iron Age hillfort at Cadbury Castle thus rest in the overall range of AD 45–61. It appears that the archaeological evidence is not able to narrow this range, nor does the historical evidence allow a closer date. The chronological problems are largely of historical interpretation, and unless archaeology can refine the chronology of some of the artefacts crucial for this particular question, the chronology is likely to remain based on history. The choice of an earlier or later date for the massacre rests on the interpretation of the historical circumstances and probabilities. The suggestion of the Boudiccan date of about AD 60 or 61 for the catastrophe was occasioned by the archaeological evidence and reinforced by historical possibility. To support it, one has to suggest that the site was somehow allied or surrendered to the Romans at the time of the initial conquest in AD 45, and that something caused it to revolt at the time of the Boudiccan rebellion. Although it is perhaps easier from an historical point of view to group the destruction at Cadbury Castle with those that occurred in the first wave of the Roman invasion under Vespasian, most scholars seem to have accepted the later scenario.[34]

Chapter 5

Interpreting the evidence

As has been outlined above, archaeological finds can be dated by various means, including the use of historical, archaeological, and, when appropriate, scientific evidence. An example for the Roman world has been given in the last chapter of the way in which all these categories of evidence were used to determine a date for an event revealed by excavation. In the case of the Cadbury massacre, it was a question of a choice between two historically-possible dates. The archaeological evidence proved to be the decisive factor, leading virtually all the authorities to accept the later date rather than an earlier one that was actually more comfortable historically. An example from the Greek world also involves the choice between two dates derived from historical sources, but the interpretation of the archaeological evidence leads to disagreement between scholars.

One of the most important archaeological finds of the last twenty years was the discovery and excavation of three tombs (two unlooted) at the site of Vergina in Macedonia, northern Greece. The archaeological evidence and the historical evidence for the period coincide to the point that agreement has been reached that these tombs are datable to the second half of the fourth century BC and are royal tombs, belonging to members of the Macedonian royal family.[1] We are relatively well-informed as to the tortured history of the period, and historians have generally agreed about the sequence of events. The major disagreement concerns the occupants (bones of both a male and a female were found), and hence the date, of the largest and best preserved tomb, Tomb Two. The historical evidence allows either Philip II, who was assassinated in 336 BC, and his wife Cleopatra, or Philip III, Arrhidaeus, and his wife, who were buried in 316 BC. The excavator has championed the first alternative, and the possibility that Tomb Two is the resting place of such a major historical personage as Philip II, the father of Alexander the Great, has perhaps provided greater excitement than is usual in chronological debates. The various arguments concerning probability based on the historical evidence, architectural forms, anthropological evidence from the bones recovered, or other concerns will not be repeated here (see note 1). Tomb Two was found unlooted with most of the funeral goods still preserved, including many objects in precious metals. This, then, can be treated as a closed deposit with the date of the latest item found in it indicating at least a time after which the burial was sealed, as outlined in the discussion of stratigraphy (p. 20). Theoretically, the large number of finds should yield examples of objects independently dated that would provide the necessary information. Unfortunately, a number of the precious objects are unique, and some of the more common types have not yet been fully published. Moreover, it must be recognized that one is dealing with an actual difference of only some twenty years, and it might be considered doubtful whether the chronology of classical archaeology for this period is able to distinguish so fine a line. One wonders if the material culture of most societies changes enough in twenty years to be archaeologically distinguishable, given a parallel situation with similar luck of burial, preservation, and discovery.

Among the scores of objects from Tomb Two, four black-glazed salt-cellars of a distinctive spool shape have been recognized as identical in shape to examples from dated contexts in the Agora at Athens; and they provide evidence for the date of the sealing of the tomb.[2] The Agora examples are shown in profile drawing in Figure 26. Each of the three come from specific deposits that are considered "closed contexts." The deposits are dated by a combination of evidence involving the excavators' observations of the make-up of the fills from which the objects came, their association with pottery dated from other deposits, and numismatic evidence. The best dated of the deposits was that for the saltcellar P3509, a well, situated near the Tholos, the building in which the Prytaneis met (see Chapter 2, p. 11). The date for this deposit rests on analysis of the composition of the fill and the coins found within it, especially one that, on the basis of recent new study, has been redated to the years between 307 and 300 BC. Its position in the lowest levels provides a date after which the well must have been filled. Other material in the well, such as roofing tiles labelled as public property, fragments of public measures, and pottery suitable for the dining undertaken by the Prytaneis, appears closely associated with the Tholos building, suggesting some destruction and subsequent cleaning up of debris, which can be associated with political disturbances during the year 295/4 BC on the basis of historical records that indicate an interruption in the Athenian government that

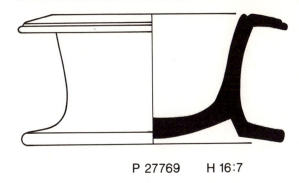

P 27769   H 16:7

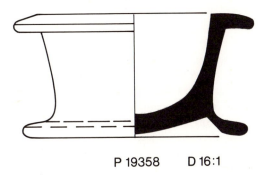

P 19358   D 16:1

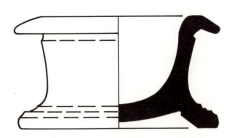

P 3509   F 11:2   (dump)

Figure 26   Profiles of spool saltcellars from the Athenian Agora, as drawn by Susan Rotroff

some modern scholars have interpreted as evidence for a *coup d'état*.[3] It is interesting to note that the kantharoi of Figure 20 in Chapter 3 (p. 53) came from this deposit and represent some seventy-five years of development from about 375 to 300 BC, indicating that apparently some relatively old pottery found its way into the well. The study of the contexts of the three Agora saltcellars leads to the conclusion that "A date between 325 and 295 would therefore be the most likely for the spool saltcellars as well."[4] The conclusion is based on several lines of reasoning: the saltcellars' state of preservation (showing little wear, suggesting they were not in use long before being deposited), the date of the bulk of the pottery that accompanied them (last quarter of the century and a few pieces of the very early third century BC), and the homogeneity of the deposits.

If Tomb Two at Vergina contained objects made between 325 and 295 BC, it cannot be the resting place of Philip II, who died in 336, but it could be the place of interment of Philip III, who was buried in 316 BC. It can still be argued, however, that the shape of the spool saltcellars might have developed earlier, and the Athenian examples could belong with the earliest pottery in the deposits rather than the later and therefore still date to the third quarter of the century.[5] Thus, evidence derived from archaeology, and the nature of the development, chronology, and distribution of styles can be viewed in different ways, depending on the interpretation put on the excavation evidence and the weight given to historical evidence. There is still no consensus of opinion as to who was buried in Tomb Two.

Although a general framework of chronology has been built up for the classical world, based on various fixed points, these can be shaky and the evidence for them open to interpretation and doubt. An awareness of just how shaky many of these are can be gained from a study of a dispute that developed in the 1980s concerning the absolute chronology of the Early Greek period. In a great many articles, notes, reviews, and a book, the late E. D. Francis and Michael Vickers challenged the prevailing chronology of the eighth through the early fifth century BC. The effect of their new chronology was a general lowering of accepted dates in this period by a maximum of as much as some sixty years so that, for instance, a number of monuments previously dated to before the Persian invasion of 480 BC are redated to later in the century. The divergence between the old system and the suggested new dates is least towards the end of this span of time, and by the middle of the fifth century BC, when there is relatively more and better chronological evidence, the new chronology once more agrees with the old chronological system. From that point on there is consensus among scholars as to the outlines of Greek chronology. A trend in recent times had been to an overall lowering of dates, but not to the extent proposed by Francis/Vickers.[6] Their suggested new chronology was a major and significant wrench to the conceptual framework of the development of Greek art and a challenge to the scholarship of the past and to most of the scholars of the present. It was not long before it was disputed.[7]

The accepted chronology is the result of basically nineteenth-century scholarship, codified in the earlier years of this century, and refined and continually adjusted down to the present day. The chronology of the early Greek period rests on a number of fixed points, many of which are destruction levels and other monuments associated with the Persian Wars, and whose dates are derived from historical references. In addition, a small number of buildings are thought to be dated by literary references, and these act as pegs on which relative chronologies are draped, as has been explained in Chapter 3 (pp. 57–60). Francis/Vickers do not dispute the relative chronologies but believe that the evidence for the absolute dates of these fixed points for the sixth century BC and earlier has been misinterpreted, misunderstood, or simply ignored, and that the fixed points should be much later than the traditional chronology allows. Their procedure is to examine each fixed point from the point of view of the evidence for its date, but it is clear that the authors have been convinced that the prevailing chronology is too high for a number of reasons, and are determined to prove their point. This necessitates redating the artistic development of 'archaic' art and also a number of major monuments to fit in with their newly-developed chronological scheme.

The basis of the Francis/Vickers chronology appears to be the belief that archaeological remains and finds should closely coincide with historical events.[8] They see a glaring contradiction between their interpretation of the historical and literary evidence of many ancient authors as to the richness of Greece derived from the spoils of the Persian Wars and the archaeological record. In order to reconcile what they see as a contradiction, they believe that many of the buildings, monuments, and even changes in styles of art, such as the invention of the red-figure style of vase-painting, were directly related to the victory over the Persians, were influenced by it, or were financed by the wealth that accrued from the victory. They also believe that much of the iconography, or subject matter of Greek art, carries secondary meaning and is also directly related to the Persian Wars. An example of this is representations of Greeks fighting Amazons, which are seen as symbolizing the battles of Greeks versus Persians and thus commemorating the Persian Wars.

These subjects should then generally appear after the Persian defeat and refer to it. Their appearance is used as one of the criteria to support the later chronology. This causes a number of works of art, originally dated in the late sixth century BC before the Persians, to be redated to after the Persian invasions, for they are seen as commemorating the Greek victory over the eastern invaders. In the case of archaeological evidence thought to represent destruction wrought by the Persians in Athens and elsewhere, other, later, historical circumstances or undocumented later enemy action are invoked to explain it. For instance, evidence for destructions in Athens and on the Acropolis is connected with internal political disturbances in the 460s BC.

The Vickers/Francis chronology has not won many adherents. Criticism has been leveled on the basis of methodology, including choice of sources, specific misunderstandings, or outright mistakes in evaluating archaeological material, misunderstanding of the dynamics of stylistic development and iconography, and inconsistencies in argument. The new chronology shifts so much material from the end of the sixth century BC to the fifth that it produces an extreme compression of time. There then also seem to be few monuments or works of art at the upper end of the scale, before the Persian invasion, if almost everything is moved to after the Persian Wars. The authors' view of the relationship of history to the physical record is a concern, and a general criticism is that Francis/Vickers are attempting to force the evidence into a preconceived scenario.

The value of the Vickers/Francis controversy is that it has forced students to re-evaluate the old chronology and look again at the evidence in light of new information and the new challenges. It is painfully clear, after working through all the evidence and arguments, that relatively few of the fixed points can stand up to a determined attack and scholarly skepticism. The sheer complexity of the issues and the lack of clear, unambiguous answers allows a great deal of room for interpretation. The evidence will often support both simple, straightforward answers and more involved scenarios. A number of points made by Francis/Vickers are certainly well taken, particularly their warning of the lingering effects of nineteenth-century romanticism as applied to ancient Greece, which can still be observed today, even among students. They have managed, in the views of some, to demolish or at least cast doubt on a number of traditional chronological fixed points, but in a great many other individual cases the evidence is just not sufficient to prove their thesis. Despite the research of some seventy years since the chronology was more or less codified and the erudite and clever arguments of Francis/Vickers, some of the older fixed points, such as the Siphnian Treasury and the mound in the Marathon plain, still remain and do not seem to have been seriously dislodged.[9] It is to be expected that, in the future, archaeology, and probably dendrochronology, will produce additional evidence, new fixed points, and new interpretations for dating that will allow further tests for the chronology of early Greece.

As has been demonstrated, matters of dating and chronology in classical archaeology are not simple nor easily understood. Relative dating depends much upon the identification and understanding of style, and the individual training and eye of the scholar must be the decisive factor. Objects, even buildings, can be ranged into relative sequences that may find general acceptance, depending of course that proper consideration is given to such matters as quality, location, speed of development and diffusion, historical evidence, etc., as outlined in Chapter 3. Assigning absolute dates is difficult and will likely remain so, unless a scientific method can attain sufficient precision to be useful for classical archaeology. Until then, absolute dating will still be a matter of the interpretation of a complex mass of circumstantial evidence both from archaeology and from the interpretation of the texts. Excavation and study will continue to produce information that will need to be evaluated by each succeeding generation, bringing its own training and background to the problems. Classical archaeology is a relatively young discipline compared to other academic fields, and the influence of its founders is beginning to fade. It is thus correct and appropriate that their ideas and solutions are questioned afresh by a new generation of scholars. This is definitely happening in the field of Greek and Roman sculpture, where many of the nineteenth-century theories and ideas are being freshly looked at and in many cases challenged. The Francis/Vickers assault on the accepted chronology of Early Iron Age Greece can be seen in this light as symptomatic of the wider movement of challenge to views inherited from earlier scholarship.

The inherent problems of dating the past that have been only briefly outlined above indicate how difficult it is to measure. Accidents of preservation and recovery, pure chance, vagaries of modern history, and human foibles all have worked to limit and to distort our knowledge and understanding of the past, and, given the violent history of the lands involved, it is quite amazing that we know as much as we do. Our ability to date something, i.e., relating objects chronologically to our own time, rests on the evidence of archaeology and the interpretation of the written record; and sometimes only on archaeology when there is no literary or historical evidence. Archaeology is not an exact science, or perhaps not a science at all, and reasonable conclusions can only be reached by a knowledgeable and unprejudiced view of the varied, and often incomplete, material with which the investigator has to work. Absolute certainty is not possible due to the nature of the evidence, and although a fundamentalist approach to the literary evidence, or to archaeological evidence for that matter, may be comforting, as are all such approaches, an investigator must try to keep an open mind and critical common sense. Often the cumulative weight of various small pieces of evidence may lead to a conclusion, and a well-trained and experienced intellect should be able to evaluate such "straws in the wind." Many times the choice is between two possibilities, and a decision must be based on which is the more likely, taking into account all the various ways of looking at the evidence. Scholarship in this field is often one of probabilities and possibilities, and as long as the evidence is so ambiguous, there will be disagreements over interpretations and "weight" of the evidence, of style, and ultimately over chronology. The question "what date is it?" will still be asked for an artefact from the classical world, and over the years we have built up a framework to answer that question in terms of our own method of time reckoning. Parts of this framework are stronger than others; some are rickety, but the structure holds together relatively well and provides some answers. These are perhaps not the precise answers that the modern technical world would like, but given the huge problems involved in knowing anything about that remote world of antiquity, we are not doing too badly and are, in fact, slowly improving our ability to date Greek and Roman art and artefacts all the time.

Notes

1 Introduction: classical archaeology and chronology

1 A short survey of the various methods of both survey and sub-surface investigations can be found in M. Joukowsky, *A Complete Manual of Field Archaeology: Tools and Techniques of Field Work for Archaeologists*, Englewood Cliffs, New Jersey, Prentice-Hall, 1980, pp. 35–131. For some of the new survey techniques, I. Scollar, *et al.*, *Archaeological Prospecting and Remote Sensing*, Cambridge, Cambridge University Press, 1990. An influential paper containing a theoretical discussion of archaeological investigation, including surface survey and analysis of data, is Charles L. Redman, "Multistage Fieldwork and Analytical Techniques," *American Antiquity*, vol. 28, no. 1, 1973, pp. 61–79.

2 An example of this activity can be found in the proceedings of the most recent conference devoted to the myriad problems surrounding the Bronze Age finds from the island of Thera: *Thera and the Aegean World: Proceedings of the Third International Congress*, vols 1–3, London, Thera Foundation, 1990. For the chronology of the Aegean Bronze Age, Peter Warren and Vronwy Hankey, *Aegean Bronze Age Chronology*, Bristol, Bristol Classical Press, 1989. A general overview from an historical perspective of the Bronze Age archaeology in Greece: W. A. McDonald and Carol G. Thomas, *Progress into the Past: The Rediscovery of Mycenaean Civilization*, 2nd edn, Bloomington and Indianapolis, Indiana, Indiana University Press, 1990. For prehistoric Italy, a short survey is provided by John Reich, *Italy Before Rome*, Oxford, Elsevier–Phaidon, 1979. See also, R. Ross Holloway, *Italy and the Aegean, 3000–700 B.C.*, Archaeologia Transatlantica I, Louvain-la Neuve (Belgium), Centre d'archéologie grecque, Université Catholique de Louvain, and Center for Old World Archaeology and Art, Brown University, 1981. An excellent survey of the various cultures that existed in the Italian peninsula between the ninth and the eighth centuries BC is Sabatino Moscati, *Italy Before Rome*, Milan, Electa, 1987. For an earlier collection of papers on the same general subject, see David and Francesca R. Ridgway, *Italy Before the Romans*, London, Academic Press, 1979.

3 The problem of the relationship of historical evidence to the archaeological record is pointed out by Anthony Snodgrass in ch. 2 of M. Crawford (ed.), *Sources for Ancient History*, Cambridge, Cambridge University Press, 1983, pp. 137–84. See also "Archaeology and History," in the same author's *An Archaeology of Greece*, Berkeley and Los Angeles, California and London,

University of California Press, 1987, pp. 36–66; for the Roman side of things, M. Todd, "Dating the Roman Empire: The Contribution of Archaeology," in B. Orme (ed.), *Problems and Case Studies in Archaeological Dating*, Exeter Studies in History, no. 4, Exeter Studies in Archaeology, no. 1, Exeter, University of Exeter, 1982, pp. 35–56; "Archaeology and History," ch. 4 in Stephen Johnson, *Rome and its Empire*, London and New York, Routledge, 1989, pp. 48–62.

4 Several good general publications have appeared recently that demonstrate clearly the sometimes remarkable detail and information that have been recovered from some of these major sites: John M. Camp, *The Athenian Agora: Excavations in the Heart of Classical Athens*, London, Thames & Hudson, 1986; Joseph Jay Deiss, *Herculaneum, Italy's Buried Treasure*, rev. and updated edn (1985), Malibu, J. Paul Getty Museum, 1989. For an example of continued interest and up-to-date scientific research in Pompeii see the exhibition catalogue, *Rediscovering Pompeii*, Rome, L'Erma di Bretschneider, 1990.

5 One of the most characteristic of all Roman building types is the bath; it occurs wherever the Romans went and can be considered one of the defining features of a Roman town. See Janet DeLaine, "Recent Research on Roman Baths," *Journal of Roman Archaeology*, 1988, vol. 1, pp. 11–32, for an indication of the kinds of information that studies of this type of building can and have produced.

6 For a basic bibliography on Greek pottery and painting, see note 11 for Chapter 3.

7 For example, the reliefs on Trajan's Column in Rome record a military expedition in some detail. See Chapter 3 (pp. 28–30) for a discussion of these reliefs and their relationship to the contemporary, but stylistically very different, sculptured relief panels from a Trajanic monument originally erected in what is now Rumania.

8 For basic bibliography on Greek and Roman oil lamps, see Chapter 3, note 19.

2 How time is recorded

1 The subject of calendars and general telling of time in the ancient world is very complex and can only be lightly touched upon in this work, which relies completely on the following studies. The best general treatment of the subject in English is E. J. Bickerman, *Chronology of the Ancient World*, 2nd edn, Ithaca, New York, Cornell University Press, 1980. A basic work is Alan E. Samuel, *Greek and Roman Chronology. Calendars and Years in Classical Antiquity (Handbuch der Altertumswissenschaft)*, vol. 1.7, Munich, Beck, 1972; a shorter version by the same author is "Calendar and Time-Telling," in Michael Grant and Rachel Kitzinger (eds), *Civilization of the Ancient Mediterranean*, vol. 1, New York, Scribner's Sons, 1988, pp. 389–95. An engagingly written survey is Hanbury Brown, "Stars and Time," ch. 2 in his *Man and the Stars*, Oxford, Oxford University Press, 1978, pp. 21–42. Chapter 7 ("Telling Time") in O. A. W. Dilke's *Mathematics and Measurement*, 2nd edn, London, British Museum, 1989, pp. 40–45 serves as a short and easy survey of the subject.

2 Dilke, op. cit., pp. 42–4 briefly covers sundials. The basic study is Sharon Gibbs, *Greek and Roman Sundials*, New Haven and London, Yale University

Press, 1976. R. R. Rohr's, *Sundials, History, Theory and Practice* (Gabriel Godin trans.), Toronto, University of Toronto Press, 1970, is an overall survey of the subject from ancient times up to the present. For the giant sundial in Rome erected by Augustus on the Campus Martius, a short discussion in English, with references to the major publications in German by the discoverer, Edmund Buchner, can be found in Anthony Snodgrass, *An Archaeology of Greece*, Berkeley and Los Angeles, California and London, University of California Press, 1987, pp. 27–31.

3 Water-clocks are also briefly treated by Dilke, op. cit., pp. 44–5. For a photo of the *klepsydra* from the Athenian lawcourts: John M. Camp, *The Athenian Agora: Excavations in the Heart of Classical Athens*, London, Thames & Hudson, 1986, p. 111, fig. 85. The Athenian Agora has also produced a larger, built water-clock that started out life as an out-flow clock in the fourth century BC but was then apparently changed into an in-flow clock. The basic publication of this construction also contains a good, short, basic explanation of the different types of water-clocks with a bibliography on the subject: Joe E. Armstrong and John McK. Camp II, "Notes on a Water Clock in the Athenian Agora," *Hesperia*, 1977, vol. 46, no. 2, pp. 147–61. Donald Hill, "Clocks," Ch. 12 in his *A History of Engineering in Classical and Medieval Times*, La Salle, Illinois, Open Court Publishing Co., 1984, pp. 223–42 deals with water-clocks from all periods and the hydraulic machinery that can be attached to them.

4 For the Athenian calendars, see Bickerman, op. cit., pp. 34–8. The basic modern works are given in his footnote 30, p. 100.

5 Thucydides 2.2.

6 Dating by the year of "the indiction" refers to tax years, the indiction being the annual assessment of taxes in kind of various types. See Bickerman, op. cit., pp. 78–9. For the interesting subject of the methods of collecting taxes in the Late Roman Empire, A. H. M. Jones, *The Later Roman Empire, 284–602. A Social, Economic, and Administrative Survey*, vol. 1, Oxford, Basil Blackwell, 1973 (report of 1964 edn), particularly pp. 448–62.

7 The inscription that is quoted in the text is on a north Syrian limestone funerary monument in the Museum of Art and Archaeology of the University of Missouri (acc. no. 70.19) and has been most recently published by Klaus Parlasca, "Syrische Grabreliefs hellenistischer und römischer Zeit: Fundgruppen und Probleme," *Trierer Winckelmannsprogramm*, vol. 3, 1981, Mainz am Rhein, Philipp von Zabern, 1982, p. 11, pl. 10.2. For all the different civil calendars and methods of reckoning time that were used in the Greek and Roman world, see Samuel, *Greek and Roman Chronology*, op. cit., pp. 57–88. There is evidence for some ninety-five Greek civil calendars!

8 An interesting problem not solved clearly in the sources is exactly when within a given year the festival would fall, see Samuel, *Greek and Roman Chronology*, op. cit., pp. 191–4.

9 Plutarch, *Parallel Lives*, "Numa Pompilius," 1.4. It is interesting to note that at the beginning of this chapter of the *Parallel Lives*, Plutarch mentions some of the problems he faced in trying to establish the correct dates for his subject. He lists disputes between sources, difficulties in the identification of characters through confusion of names, loss of documentary evidence through war, and forgeries by individuals who wanted their ancestors to appear as part of the historical record. These are, of course, some of the same problems that

historians of ancient times still face today, almost 2,000 years later.

10 An earlier eclipse recorded by Livy as having taken place on July 11, 190 BC is dated to March 14 by modern calculations. This indicates almost four months difference and suggests than an adjustment must have been made between 190 and 168 BC, which reduced the discrepancy, but only to two-and-a-half months by 168. For these dates and other synchronizations, see Samuel, *Greek and Roman Chronology*, op. cit., pp. 163–4 and the references cited therein.

11 For the history of the calendar now in general use in the western world, see N. M. Denis-Boulet, *The Christian Calendar* (P. Hepurne-Scott trans.), New York, Hawthorne Books, 1960. An overall treatment of the development of the idea of time throughout history: Stephen Toulmin and June Goodfield, *The Discovery of Time*, New York and Evanston, Illinois, Harper & Row, 1965. A popular discussion of the problems involved with time, history, and calendars can be found in Daniel J. Boorstin, *The Discoverers*, New York, Vintage Books (Random House), 1985, pp. 4–53, 558–635.

3 Relative dating

1 For the history of the development of archaeology, see Glyn Daniel, *A Short History of Archaeology*, London, Thames & Hudson, 1981.

2 For recent publications on ancient Thera and the investigations at Pompeii and Herculaneum, see Chapter 1, notes 2 and 4.

3 The Marathon mound is considered by most scholars as a dated monument, important for Greek absolute chronology. For its identification and date, see Chapter 5, note 9.

4 The section reproduced here and its interpretation are taken from the excavation report of the Agora Excavations for 1980–1982; T. Leslie Shear, Jr, "The Athenian Agora: Excavations of 1980–1982," *Hesperia*, 1984, vol. 53, pp. 1–57 (for the section, p. 52, fig. 18). Appreciation goes to Professor Shear and to the secretary of the Agora Excavations, Mrs Jan Diamant, for providing the section drawing.

5 This project is a collaborative excavation by the Soprintendenza Archeologica di Roma and the American Academy in Rome. Special thanks are due to the Director of the Excavations, Eric Hostetter, for providing the information and arranging for the section to be drawn specifically for this book, and to Thomas Howe, Associate Director of the "Palatine East" excavation, who worked under some difficulties to accomplish that task. Preliminary excavation reports appear yearly in *Bollettino di Archeologia* and approximately every two years in the *Memoirs of the American Academy in Rome*.

6 For Trajan's Column, the best treatment in English is Lino Rossi, *Trajan's Column and the Dacian Wars*, London, Thames & Hudson, 1971; for the "metopes" of the Tropaeum Traiani, *idem.*, "A Historiographic Reassessment of the Metopes of the Tropaeum Traiani at Adamklissi,"*Archaeological Journal*, 1972, vol. 129, pp. 56–68. The basic publication of the monument, with clear illustrations of all the sculpture: F. B. Florescu, *Das Siegesdenkmal von Adamklissi. Tropaeum Traiani*, Bonn, Habelt, 1965.

7 A good example of the difficulties involved in dating by style can be given by Roman bronze relief mirrors, a category of objects that is not dated by

external evidence. The relief decoration was made by hammering bronze sheets down into a metal or stone matrix that had the scene cut into it. A number of these decorated mirrors exist with a limited repertory of scenes decorating them. The problems arise when there are variations in form between the representations on the mirrors. Are the differences to be accounted for by date or by some other factors, such as those mentioned above? An individual mirror dated some fifty years later than others by one scholar can be thought to be dated together with them by another. For a discussion of the type, the problems of dating it, and the view that all these mirrors are likely to belong to about the middle of the second century AD, Elizabeth Milleker, "The Three Graces on a Roman Relief Mirror," *Metropolitan Museum Journal*, 1988, vol. 23, pp. 69–81.

8 For Greek architecture, the basic handbooks are: W. B. Dinsmoor, *The Architecture of Ancient Greece*, 3rd edn, London and New York, Batsford, 1952; D. S. Robertson, *Greek and Roman Architecture*, 2nd edn, Cambridge, Cambridge University Press, 1969; A. W. Lawrence, *Greek Architecture*, rev. by R. A. Tomlinson, Harmondsworth, Penguin Books, 1983. Also, see J. J. Coulton, *Ancient Greek Architects at Work*, Ithaca, New York, Cornell University Press, 1977. For Roman architecture: J. B. Ward-Perkins, *Roman Imperial Architecture*, Harmondsworth, Penguin Books, 1981; Frank Sear, *Roman Architecture*, Ithaca, New York, Cornell University Press, 1982; William L. MacDonald, *The Architecture of the Roman Empire, I, An Introductory Study*, rev. edn, New Haven, Connecticut and London, Yale University Press, 1982; idem., *The Architecture of the Roman Empire, II, An Urban Appraisal*, New Haven, Connecticut and London, Yale University Press, 1986. A recent overall history of architecture is Spiro Kostoff, *A History of Architecture*, New York, Oxford University Press, 1985. For post-modern architecture and its relationship to the past, see ibid., pp. 752–5.

9 For questions of form and proportions, see Coulton, op. cit., pp. 97–123, and especially pp. 104–8 on the Doric capital. The interpretation of the development of the Doric capital given here is based on a technical study by Coulton that analyzes 214 capitals: "Doric Capitals: A Proportional Analysis," *The Annual of the British School at Athens*, 1979, vol. 74, pp. 81–153. An example of how an architect might not follow plans slavishly but modify them in the process of construction has recently been documented from the site of Didyma, on the coast of present-day Turkey. Here actual one-to-one plans of the Temple of Apollo have been identified scratched on the unfinished walls of the building. The measurements of some of the still preserved elements of the building, for instance the Ionic column bases, do not always coincide exactly with their elevations as recorded on the walls, and it appears that the proportions of the bases were changed in the course of construction, probably by the architect in charge; Lothar Haselberger, "The Construction Plans of the Temple of Apollo at Didyma," *Scientific American*, 1985, vol. n.s. 253, no. 6 (December), pp. 126–32. For more detailed discussions of these newly discovered drawings, see Haselberger's reports in the *Istanbuler Mitteilungen*, 1980, vol. 30, pp. 191–215; 1983, vol. 33, pp. 90–123.

10 The bibliography on Greek and Roman sculpture is immense. Still useful for an overview of both subjects is A. W. Lawrence, *Greek and Roman Sculpture*, New York, Harper & Row, 1972; George M. A. Hanfmann, *Classical Sculpture*,

London, George Rainbird Ltd, 1967. For Greek sculpture the latest overview is Andrew Stewart, *Greek Sculpture*, New Haven, Connecticut and London, Yale University Press, 1990. A short and useful survey is John Barron, *An Introduction to Greek Sculpture*, London, Athlone Press, 1981; and still basic is Gisela M. A. Richter, *The Sculpture and Sculptors of the Greeks*, 4th rev. edn, New Haven, Connecticut and London, Yale University Press 1970. There are also a number of specific studies either by period or by type of sculpture by Richter, John Boardman, and B. S. Ridgway, references to which can be found in Stewart. Recent new studies are Brunhilde Sismondo Ridgway, *Hellenistic Sculpture I*, Madison, Wisconsin, University of Wisconsin Press, 1990, and R. R. R. Smith, *Hellenistic Sculpture*, London, Thames & Hudson, 1991. Roman sculpture has not received such attention in English. See Richard Brilliant, *Roman Art*, London, Phaidon, 1974, chs 2–6; Donald Strong, *Roman Art*, Harmondsworth, Penguin Books, 1976, *passim*; Anthony Bonanno, "Sculpture," in Martin Henig (ed.), *A Handbook of Roman Art*, Ithaca, New York, Cornell University Press, 1983, pp. 66–96; D. E. Strong, *Roman Imperial Sculpture*, London, Alec Tiranti, 1961. The most recent general handbook for Roman art treats sculpture in a clear, chronological manner: Nancy H. Ramage and Andrew Ramage, *Roman Art: Romulus to Constantine*, New York, Harry N. Abrams, 1991. An interesting approach to dating can be found in K. D. Morrow, *Greek Footwear and the Dating of Sculpture*, Madison, Wisconsin, University of Wisconsin Press, 1985.

11 For Greek painting on pottery, the basic handbook has been R. M. Cook, *Greek Painted Pottery*, 2nd edn, London, Methuen, 1972. New overall treatments of Greek pottery are Tom Rasmussen and Nigel Spivey (eds), *Looking at Greek Vases*, Cambridge and New York, Cambridge University Press, 1991, and Brian A. Sparkes, *Greek Pottery: an introduction*, Manchester and New York, Manchester University Press, 1991. Copiously illustrated handbooks dealing with the leading school, that of Attica, have been published by John Boardman; *Athenian Black Figure Vases*, London, Thames & Hudson, 1974; *Athenian Red Figure Vases. The Archaic Period*, London, Thames & Hudson, 1975; *Athenian Red Figure Vases. The Classical Period*, London, Thames & Hudson, 1989. Among many studies of individual schools or painters, the latest study of Corinthian is D. A. Amyx, *Corinthian Vase-Painting of the Archaic Period*, Berkeley, California, University of California Press, 1988. For monumental painting: Vincent J. Bruno, *Form and Color in Greek Painting*, New York, Norton, 1977. The whole topic of Greek painting is also well treated in Martin Robertson, *Greek Painting*, Geneva, Skira, 1959. For the huge subject of Roman painting, Roger Ling, *Roman Painting*, Cambridge, Cambridge University Press, 1991; a shorter treatment with extensive bibliography is Joan Liversidge, "Wall Painting and Stucco," ch. 4 in Martin Henig (ed.), *A Handbook of Roman Art*, Ithaca, New York, Cornell University Press, 1983, pp. 97–115; also useful for a large number of illustrations but with a slim text is Arturo Stenico, *Roman and Etruscan Painting*, New York, Viking Press, 1963.

12 Museum of Art and Archaeology, University of Missouri, acc. no. 60.13, Chorn Memorial Fund Purchase.

13 A good discussion of the red-figure and the black-figure techniques is to be found in J. M. Hurwit, *The Art and Culture of Early Greece, 1100–480 B.C.*, Ithaca, New York and London, Cornell University Press, 1985, pp. 280–92.

14 The detail, Figure 18, is from a pyxis, a small box used perhaps for toilet articles and trinkets, in the Art Institute of Chicago, Museum Purchase Fund, 1905.343.

15 For a short and informative survey of typological changes in common Attic pottery, see Brian A. Sparkes and Lucy Talcott in *The Athenian Agora, Results of the Excavations Conducted by the American School of Classical Studies at Athens, vol. XII, Black and Plain Pottery*, Princeton, New Jersey, American School of Classical Studies at Athens, 1970, part I, pp. 9–12.

16 Museum of Art and Archaeology, University of Missouri, acc. no. 62.12, Alumni Achievement Fund. This olpe has been assigned to the Etruscan site of Vulci in Italy and attributed to the early sixth-century "Vulci Masters" by J. Szilágyi. For a short discussion with bibliography of the Etrusco-Corinthian painting style and its relationship to Corinthian, see W. Biers, "An Etruscan Face: a Mask Cup in Missouri," *Muse*, 1979, vol. 13, pp. 45–53; for the olpe's attribution, p. 53, note 10.

17 The photo, Figure 20, is a cropped version of the photo appearing on plate 67 of Susan Rotroff's article, "Spool Saltcellars in the Athenian Agora," *Hesperia*, 1984, vol. 53, no. 3, pp. 343–54. For the dating of the kantharoi, ibid., pp. 348–9, 353.

18 The establishment of the stylistic development of the conical loom-weight was worked out by Gladys R. Davidson in *Corinth, Results of Excavations Conducted by the American School of Classical Studies at Athens, vol. XII, The Minor Arts*, Princeton, New Jersey, American School of Classical Studies at Athens, 1952, pp. 147–72. The following dates, expressed in the more or less generalized terms necessary for the material and the evidence, are assigned to the profiles: Profile I, late eighth and early seventh century BC; II, later, but not later than 625 BC; III, sixth century and early part of the fifth; IV, late sixth century; V, early fifth century to about 480 BC; VI, contemporary with V; VII, starts perhaps a decade later than VI to before 450 BC; VIII, mid-fifth century to the end of the century; IX, 400–350 BC; X, 350–300 BC; XI, developed between 300–250 BC, died out perhaps near the end of third century; XII, XIII, 250–146 BC; XIV, about 200 BC.

A short description with a bibliography on the craft of weaving and cloth production in antiquity can be found in J. P. Wild, "Textiles," ch. 13 in Donald Strong and David Brown (eds), *Roman Crafts*, New York, New York University Press, 1976, pp. 166–77.

19 A short but very useful treatment of the lamps from the Athenian Agora is to be found in J. Perlzweig, *Lamps from the Athenian Agora*, Excavations at the Athenian Agora, Picture Book, 9, Princeton, New Jersey, American School of Classical Studies, 1963. Figures 22–4 here are figures 74–121 in this work. Also for lamps, see D. M. Bailey, *A Catalogue of the Lamps in the British Museum*, vols 1–3, London, British Museum Publications, 1975–1988; and *idem.*, "Lamps Metal, Lamps Clay: A Decade of Publication," *Journal of Roman Archaeology*, 1991, vol. 4, pp. 51–62.

4 Absolute dating

1 There is a considerable bibliography on the subject of the methods, theory, and practice of history and historiography. For a general overview:

R. G. Collingwood, *The Idea of History*, Oxford, Clarendon Press, 1946 (see particularly part I, "Greco-Roman Historiography," pp. 14–42); Matthew Fitzsimons, Alfred Pundt and Charles Nowell (eds), *The Development of Historiography*, Harrisburg, Pennsylvania, Stackpole Company, 1954. The ancient world is surveyed in ch. 1, "The Heritage of Antiquity," by Karl Dannenfeldt. Also of interest: M. I. Finley, *Ancient History*, London, Chatto & Windus, 1985; Hermann Bengtson, *Introduction to Ancient History*, 6th edn (R. L. Frank and D. Gillard trans.), Berkeley and Los Angeles, California, University of California Press, 1970.

A very useful summary of the sources for ancient history, including litera-ture as well as archaeology, inscriptions, and coins, is M. Crawford (ed.), *Sources for Ancient History*, Cambridge, Cambridge University Press, 1983.

2 Stephen Johnson, *Rome and its Empire*, London and New York, Routledge, 1989, p. 58.

3 For recent discussions dealing with the question of the relationship of archae-ology and history, see Chapter 1, note 3.

4 The date of the destruction of the northern Greek city of Olynthus by Philip II in 348 BC has been regarded as a set point for all the material found there in the excavations that were undertaken in the 1920s and 1930s, and as such has been used as a chronological point for the development of pottery and other categories of material. Recent work has suggested that the destruction may not have been as complete as one gathers from the ancient sources and that a certain amount of material may indeed date to after 348 BC. The subject of the dating of the material from Olynthus and its ramifications for chronology was the subject of a colloquium at the Annual Meeting of the Archaeological Institute of America in 1989. For the abstracts of the papers delivered at this meeting, see the *American Journal of Archaeology*, 1990, vol. 94, no. 2, pp. 314–16.

5 Homer as an historical source is a prime example of the question of the extent to which a literary source may or may not reflect actual history, and this subject has been debated ever since the poems themselves were written. For the most recent summary of the state of this subject, see W. A. McDonald and C. G. Thomas, *Progress into the Past: The Rediscovery of Mycenaean Civilization*, 2nd edn, Bloomington and Indianapolis, Indiana, University of Indiana Press, 1990, especially pp. 465–72. For a sensible statement of what periods are represented in the epics and to what extent, J. M. Hurwit, *The Art and Culture of Early Greece, 1100–480 B. C.*, Ithaca, New York and New York, Cornell University Press, 1985, pp. 46–53. Also, Emilio Gabba, "Literature," in Crawford, op. cit., pp. 26–33. On this general subject, see W. G. Dever, "Archaeology and the Bible: Understanding the Special Relationship," *Biblical Archaeology Review*, 1990, vol. 16, no. 3, pp. 52–62.

6 Robert R. Newton, *Ancient Astronomical Observations and the Accelerations of the Earth and Moon*, Baltimore, Maryland and London, Johns Hopkins University Press, 1970, p. xiii. An easily understandable primer on astronomy is Patrick Moore, *The Amateur Astronomer*, 7th rev. edn, London, Lutterworth Press, 1971.

7 Herodotus 1.74.

8 For a discussion of the reliability of ancient eclipse records, see Newton, op. cit., pp. 35–47.

9 Thucydides, 6.3–5.

10 For a discussion of the passage in Thucydides that deals with the foundation of the western colonies, see A. W. Gomme, A. Andrewes, and K. J. Dover, *A Historical Commentary on Thucydides*, vol. IV, Oxford, Clarendon Press, 1970, pp. 198–210. A recent discussion of the Sicilian colony dates in relationship to the chronology of Corinthian pottery can be found in D. A. Amyx, *Corinthian Vase-Painting of the Archaic Period*, vol. II, Berkeley, California, University of California Press, 1988, ch. 3, pp. 397–434. For a recent summary of the Greek colonies in Sicily, see R. Ross Holloway, *The Archaeology of Ancient Sicily*, London and New York, Routledge, 1991, chs 2 and 3.

11 Sources for Greek and Roman art are conveniently drawn together in J. J. Pollitt's two works, *The Art of Ancient Greece: Sources and Documents*, Cambridge and New York, Cambridge University Press, 1990, and *The Art of Rome: Sources and Documents*, Cambridge and New York, Cambridge University Press, 1983. See also by the same author, *The Ancient View of Greek Art. Criticism, History, and Terminology*, New Haven, Connecticut and London, Yale University Press, 1974.

12 The inscriptions were either inked on the surface or inscribed after the pot was fired. Although these vases were originally thought to have been made in Alexandria, recent scientific analysis of their fabric indicates that some were made on Crete and apparently imported to Alexandria where the inscriptions were added: P. J. Callaghan and R. E. Jones, "Hadra Hydriae and Central Crete: A Fabric Analysis," *Annual of the British School at Athens*, 1985, vol. 80, pp. 1–17.

13 The sheer volume of epigraphic evidence has spawned a huge bibliography, which grows rapidly as new inscriptions are found and new and amended readings of old texts are published. For the epigraphy of the Greco-Roman civilization in general; Fergus Millar, "Epigraphy," in Crawford, op. cit., pp. 80–136. For Greek inscriptions, the basic introductory handbook in English is A. G. Woodhead, *The Study of Greek Inscriptions*, 2nd edn, Cambridge, Cambridge University Press, 1981. Criteria for the dating of inscriptions, from which our short discussion is taken, are given on pp. 52–66. More recent is B. F. Cook, *Greek Inscriptions*, London, British Museum Publications, 1987. A short overview of Greek inscriptions and what they can tell us about architecture is R. Scranton, "Greek Architectural Inscriptions as Documents," *Harvard Library Bulletin*, 1960, vol. 14, no. 2, pp. 159–82. For Roman epigraphy, the old, basic text is J. E. Sandys, *Latin Epigraphy: An Introduction to the Latin Inscriptions of the Roman World* (2nd edn, 1927, revised by S. G. Campbell), Chicago, Illinois, Ares Publishers, 1974. See also the more recent Arthur E. Gordon, *Illustrated Introduction to Latin Epigraphy*, Berkeley, California, University of California Press, 1983; and A. E. and J. S. Gordon, *Album of Dated Latin Inscriptions*, vols 1–4, Berkeley, California, University of California Press, 1958–1965.

14 Numismatics is, like epigraphy, more or less of a specialty within classical studies. Good introductions are P. Grierson, *Numismatics*, New York and London, Oxford University Press, 1975; and L. R. Laing, *Coins and Archaeology*, London, Weidenfeld & Nicolson, 1969. Particularly useful is ch. 2 in Laing on chronology, pp. 19–51. For Greek coins, a basic survey is G. K. Jenkins, *Ancient Greek Coins*, 2nd rev. edn, London, Seaby, 1990; for Roman,

C. H. V. Sutherland, *Roman Coins*, London, Barrie & Jenkins, 1974; H. Mattingly, *Roman Coins, from the Earliest Times to the Fall of the Roman Empire*, 2nd rev. edn, Chicago, Illinois, Quadrangle Books, 1960.

15 The Snettisham treasure was described by Dr Catherine Johns at a symposium on ancient jewelry held at Indiana University in September 1991. A brief report of the hoard appeared immediately after it was found: S. S. Frere, "Roman Britain in 1985," *Britannia*, 1986, vol. 17, pp. 403–4. I am indebted to Dr Johns for allowing me to use the information in the abstract of her paper and for the reference to the first publication. A full study of the treasure is in preparation. The area continues to produce hoards containing metalwork: I. M. Stead, "The Snettisham Treasure: Excavations in 1990," *Antiquity*, 1991, vol. 65, no. 248, pp. 447–65.

16 A very useful summary by Michael Crawford, "Numismatics," of the value of coins for history can be found in Crawford, op. cit., pp. 185–233. For the kinds of information even illegible coins may provide, see Alan Walker, "Worn and Corroded Coins: Their Importance for the Archaeologist," *Journal of Field Archaeology*, 1976, vol. 3, no. 3, pp. 329–34.

17 V. R. Grace, *Amphoras and the Ancient Wine Trade*, Excavations at the Athenian Agora, Picture Book no. 6, Princeton, New Jersey, American School of Classical Studies, 1961, is an excellent short introduction to the question of amphora stamps and chronology. For a clear exposition of how dated amphora handles, together with other evidence, can provide a date for an ancient building, see V. R. Grace, "The Middle Stoa Dated by Amphora Stamps," *Hesperia*, 1985, vol. 54, pp. 1–54, particularly p. 3, note 2 that discusses revisions in chronology and provides additional bibliography. The illustrated stamp, Figure 25, was attributed by Grace (private communication) and is in the Museum of Art and Archaeology, University of Missouri, acc. no. 68.136. For the dating of the name, Grace, "The Middle Stoa...," op. cit., pp. 8–9.

18 The chronological interpretation of kalos names was an important part of earlier scholars' study of the chronology of Athenian vase-painting. Recent scholarship has tended to see little dating value in kalos names. The major difficulties are pointed out by E. D. Francis and Michael Vickers, "Leagros Kalos," *Proceedings of the Cambridge Philological Society*, 1987, vol. 207, n.s., no. 27, pp. 96–136.

19 The most readable account of ostracism and the ostraca remains Eugene Vanderpool, "Ostracism at Athens," in C. G. Boulter, D. W. Bradeen *et al.* (eds), *Lectures in Memory of Louise Taft Semple, II*, University of Cincinnati Classical Studies, no. 2, Norman, Oklahoma, University of Oklahoma Press, 1973, pp. 217–70.

20 A short discussion of sling bullets can be found in C. Foss, "A Bullet of Tissaphernes," *Journal of Hellenic Studies*, 1975, vol. 95, pp. 25–30. For a number of good illustrations of bullets and a mold: Jean-Yves Empereur, "Collection Paul Canellopoulos (XVII): petits objets inscrits," *Bulletin de correspondance hellénique*, 1981, vol. 105, part 1, pp. 555–61. A general account of the sling: M. Korfmann, "The Sling as a Weapon," *Scientific American*, 1973, vol. 229, no. 4, pp. 34–42.

21 For the ancient references, Thucydides 4.12.1; Pausanias 1.15.4. The shield is published by T. L. Shear, "A Spartan Shield from Pylos," *Archaiologike*

Ephemeris, 1937, part A, pp. 140–3; see also John M. Camp, *The Athenian Agora: Excavations in the Heart of Classical Athens*, London, Thames & Hudson, 1986, pp. 71–2. For the round, hoplite shield and its development, or lack of development: Anthony Snodgrass, *Early Greek Armour and Weapons from the end of the Bronze Age to 600 B. C.*, Edinburgh, Edinburgh University Press, 1964, pp. 61–8.

22 An example of this comes from excavations at the edge of the Roman Empire, at Mirobriga in modern Portugal, where a coin of the Roman emperor Antoninus Pius, minted between AD 155/6–157/8, was found sealed in the packing of a floor of a room in a building that was part of a Roman bath complex at the site. This find produced chronological evidence that aided in determining building sequences for this particular room, and for the building of which it was a part, and it provided a set chronological point for the bath complex as a whole. W. Biers (ed.), *Mirobriga. Investigations at an Iron Age and Roman Site in Southern Portugal by the University of Missouri-Columbia, 1981–1986* Oxford, British Archaeological Reports, International Series 451, 1988, pp. 85–8, 108–12, 183–4.

23 Still basic, but out-of-date, are: D. Brothwell and E. Higgs, *Science in Archaeology*, 2nd rev. edn, New York, Praeger, 1970, "Section I, Dating," pp. 35–108; H. Michael and E. Ralph (eds), *Dating Techniques for the Archaeologist*, Cambridge, Massachusetts, MIT Press, 1971; J. Michels, *Dating Methods in Archaeology*, New York and London, Seminar Press, 1973. More recent are M. Joukowsky, *A Complete Manual of Field Archaeology: Tools and Techniques of Field Work for Archaeologists*, Englewood Cliffs, New Jersey, Prentice-Hall, 1980, ch. 18, pp. 443–56, and M. J. Aitken, *Science-based Dating in Archaeology*, London and New York, Longman, 1990. The European Science Foundation also published in the 1980s a series of short pamphlets on scientific dating techniques in the series *Handbooks for Archaeologists*: no. 1, *Thermoluminescence Dating*, 1983, no. 2, *Dendrochronological Dating*, 1984, and no. 3, *Radiocarbon Dating*, 1984. No. 4 in the series is *Archaeobotany*, 1989.

24 For a discussion of the technique, see Sheridan Bowman, *Radiocarbon Dating*, London, British Museum, 1990. The latest calibration scale for carbon-14 dates and those derived from dendrochronology can be found in *Radiocarbon*, 1986, vol. 28, no. 2B, pp. 805–1030.

25 A new extension to about 10,500 years before the present has been reported but not yet published. (Personal communication from P. I. Kuniholm.)

26 For the Trier bridge, Ulrich Leute, *Archaeometry*, Weinheim, VCH, 1987, pp. 41–2, fig. 3.3. For general descriptions of the technique, Michels, op. cit., pp. 115–29; M. G. L. Baillie, *Tree-Ring Dating and Archaeology*, Chicago, Illinois, University of Chicago Press, 1982; F. H. Schweingruber, *Tree Rings: Basics and Applications of Dendrochronology*, Dordrecht, Kluwer, 1988. On the European oak chronology, M. G. L. Baillie and D. M. Brown, "An Overview of Oak Chronologies," in E. A. Slater and J. O. Tate (eds), *Science and Archaeology, Glasgow 1987*, Oxford, British Archaeological Reports, British Series, no. 196, part ii, 1988, pp. 543–8.

27 It is unfortunately possible to radiate clay objects so that false readings can be obtained, so even thermoluminescence determinations for authenticity can possibly be suspect. Thermoluminescence tests also require a hole to be drilled in the object to obtain samples of the fabric, an exercise frowned upon

by some curators. An explanation of the technique can be found in Michels, op. cit., pp. 189–200, and a fuller and more technical account in M. J. Aitken, *Thermoluminescence Dating*, London, Academic Press, 1985; for the 130-year error limit, p. 24. The Romano-British pottery studies used more than a single sample, which is preferable, and reported a deviation of less than 5 per cent: G. A. Wagner, *Thermoluminescence Dating* (*Handbooks for Archaeologists*, no. 1), Strasbourg, 1984, p. 32.

28 The major publication of the results of this excavation is Leslie Alcock, *'By South Cadbury is that Camelot...' The Excavations of Cadbury Castle 1966–1970*, London, Thames & Hudson, 1972. The following information is taken directly from this volume.

29 For a photo of the projectile point as found, a macabre but evocative object from the site of Maiden Castle, and a description of the finds from the "war cemetery" there, see the excavation report, R. E. M. Wheeler, *Maiden Castle, Dorset*, Society of Antiquaries, Research Report 12, London, Society of Antiquaries, 1943, pl. 58A and pp. 61–8, 351–60. Wheeler suggested that the iron projectile point may have been a mass-produced catapult bolt, although it lacks the characteristic shape of Roman bolts (Wheeler, ibid., p. 281); examples of this type were also found in the levels associated by the excavator with the Roman assault at this site.

30 Alcock, op. cit., pp. 160–1.

31 ibid., pp. 170–2.

32 As reported by Manning, who presents the reasoning for the later date. W. H. Manning, 'The Conquest of the West Country,' in Keith Branigan and P. J. Fowler (eds), *The Roman West Country*, Newton Abbot, David & Charles Ltd, 1976, pp. 37–9.

33 J. A. Campbell, M. S. Baxter, and Leslie Archer, "Radiocarbon Dates for the Cadbury Massacre," *Antiquity*, 1979, vol. 53, no. 207, pp. 31–8. This article also fully describes the limitations of the method when trying to date a single archaeological event. For a more technical account of the carbon-14 dates from Cadbury Castle and a discussion of the method and its uses for archaeology, see R. E. Taylor, *Radiocarbon Dating: An Archaeological Perspective*, Orlando, Florida, Academic Press, 1987, pp. 136–46.

34 Those favoring the later date: Graham Webster, *The Roman Invasion of Britain*, London, Batsford, 1980, p. 108; Peter Salway, *Roman Britain*, Oxford, Clarendon Press, 1981, p. 121; John Peddie, *Invasion – The Roman Invasion of Britain in the Year A D 43 and the Events Leading to their Occupation of the West Country*, Gloucester, Alan Sutton Publishers, 1987, p. 148; Plantagenet Somerset Fry, *Roman Britain*, Newton Abbot, David & Charles Ltd, 1984, p. 48. In favor of the earlier date would appear to be Sheppard Frere, *A History of Roman Britain*, 3rd rev. edn, London and New York, Routledge & Kegan Paul, 1987, p. 58.

5 Interpreting the evidence

1 For a general discussion by the excavator of the tombs: Manolis Andronikos, *Vergina. The Royal Tombs and the Ancient City*, Athens, Ekdotike Athenon, 1984. A recent, fair treatment of the chronological problems can be found in Eugene N. Borza, *In the Shadow of Olympus*, Princeton, New Jersey, Princeton University Press, 1990, pp. 256–66.

2 Susan I. Rotroff, "Royal Saltcellars from the Athenian Agora," *American Journal of Archaeology*, 1982, vol. 86, no. 2, p. 283 (abstract); *idem.*, "Spool Saltcellars in the Athenian Agora," *Hesperia*, 1984, vol. 53, no. 3, pp. 343–54. I must thank Prof. Rotroff for discussing this subject with me.

3 For a discussion of the historical evidence with full bibliography, see Rotroff, "Spool Saltcellars . . . ," op. cit., pp. 345–6.

4 ibid., p. 351.

5 Andronikos, op. cit., p. 222, places the saltcellars with the earliest material in the deposits, some of which at least seems to be early enough. He does not address the numismatic evidence.

6 The lack of definitive, or at least good, chronological markers for the Early Iron Age allows a lot of discussion and controversy as it is, and suggestions for re-evaluation across the board have not been wanting. See P. J. James, I. J. Thorpe, *et al.*, "Bronze to Iron Age Chronology in the Old World: Time for Reassessment?," *Studies in Ancient Chronology*, vol. 1, London, Institute of Archaeology, University of London, 1987. Peter James, *et al.*, *Centuries of Darkness*, London, Jonathan Cape, 1991 is a continuation, in collaboration with the same scholars, of the arguments set forth in the earlier publication. It came to hand too late to be fully evaluated for this work, but the thrust seems to be that the Greek Dark Ages (between about 1200 and 900 BC) are an artificial insertion into history and did not exist; the Bronze Age ends in the eastern Mediterranean as late as about 950 BC rather than 1200 BC. It is interesting to note, in passing, that the authors believe that the reduction in dates proposed by the Francis/Vickers chronology is too drastic (ibid., p. 359, note 11).

7 The publications of Francis/Vickers on the subject of their new chronology appeared in many different places between 1981 and 1990, and even keeping track of them and others that were often inaccurately announced is a study in itself. Probably the first article that received a great amount of attention was " 'Signa priscae artis': Eretria and Siphnos," *Journal of Hellenic Studies*, 1983, vol. 183, pp. 49–67. This was followed by a number of other works of which the article by Vickers alone, "Dates, Methods and Icons," in C. Bérard (ed.), *Actes du Colloque international 'Images et société en Grèce ancienne: l'iconographie comme méthode d'analyse', 1984*, Lausanne, Institut d'archéologie et d'histoire ancienne, Université de Lausanne, 1987, pp. 19–25, perhaps gives the clearest statement of the new chronology. A posthumous book by Francis, who died in 1987, is based on lectures given in 1983 and edited by Vickers; it contains another summary of their views, and the bibliography appears to have a full listing of all their various writings on the subject: E. D. Francis, *Image and Idea in Fifth-Century Greece: Art and Literature after the Persian Wars*, London and New York, Routledge, 1990.

The first written response seems not to have appeared until 1984: John Boardman, "Signa tabulae priscae artis," *Journal of Hellenic Studies*, 1984, vol. 104, pp. 161–3. There followed a number of rebuttals of particular parts of the new chronology or overall evaluations of it, largely negative, by several scholars, and references to most of these can be found in the most recent survey of the chronology, R. M. Cook, "The Francis–Vickers Chronology," *Journal of Hellenic Studies*, 1989, vol. 109, pp. 164–70. To be added to the references contained therein is M. C. Root, "Evidence from Persepolis for the Dating of Persian and Archaic Greek Coinage," *Numismatic Chronicle*, 1988, vol. 148, pp. 1–12, which follows an article by Vickers, "Early Greek Coinage, a Reassessment," that appeared in the same journal in 1985 (vol. 145, pp. 1–44). Cook cites a number of additional fixed points, of greater or lesser solidity, that Francis/Vickers did not consider.

8 "Rather, we must not rest until both history and archaeology tell the same, consistent, story, for only then can the images we wish to study begin to make sense," Vickers, in Bérard, op. cit., p. 20.

9 The date of the Siphnian Treasury at Delphi is rooted in Herodotus' account (3.57–58) of the invasion of Siphnos by Samian exiles at approximately the same time as the Persian Cambyses was invading Egypt, which we know from Near Eastern evidence was in his fifth regnal year, around 525 BC. It is generally thought that the island could not have afforded such a costly and elaborate offering after that time, so the building is usually dated to just before the Samian attack when Siphnos was at the height of its prosperity, according to Herodotus. The elaborately decorated and well-preserved building known as the Siphnian Treasury was excavated by French archaeologists between 1892 and 1894 and so identified by its position on the route of Pausanias. Its date is generally taken as an important set point for the development of architecture, sculpture, and painting. Portions of the sculptural frieze that adorned the building show such similarities to the work of one of the first vase-painters in Athens to work in the red-figure technique, the Andocides Painter, that the Treasury's date has been used to fix the time of the invention of red-figure vase-painting. For the beginnings of red-figure painting and the artists who worked at the same time in the new medium as well as the old, see Beth Cohen, *Attic Bilingual Vases and Their Painters*, New York and London, Garland Publishing, 1978, pp. 113–17.

Francis/Vickers down-date the Treasury to the 470s BC. They first suggested that it might have been completed after the date derived from Herodotus, and then Vickers in 1985, and still in 1990 (in Francis, op. cit., p. 123, note 72), conjectured that the present building is not the Siphnian Treasury at all and has been misidentified. This allows Herodotus to be correct in his date of some other building, not yet discovered or identified; the present building wrongly called the Siphnian Treasury is thus severed from Herodotus and allowed the late date of the new chronology. The final French architectural report on the building, only published in 1987, suggests, however, an uninterrupted building program lasting only three to four years and reveals that a major part of the walls of the building were actually built of a marble distinct from that employed in any other walls in Delphi. This marble came from the island of Siphnos itself. (Georges Daux and Erik Hansen, *Fouilles de Delphes II. Topographie et architecture. Le trésor de Siphnos*, Paris, De Boccard, 1987, pp. 26–7.) It would seem unlikely that Siphnos would provide marble for someone else's building, and two treasuries for the island seem excessive.

According to Herodotus (6.117.1) and Pausanias (1.29.4; 1.32.3–5) the 192 Athenians who perished at the battle of Marathon in 490 BC were interred where they fell. A large mound in the Marathon plain was dug into in the last century by Heinrich Schliemann, who found only fragments of prehistoric pottery. Later excavation by the Greek scholar V. Stais revealed a layer of ashes, burnt human bones, and pottery, including pots painted in the black-figure technique and one stylistically relatively advanced red-figure fragment. Although the evidence is certainly not as clear as the purist would wish (there were a number of pots found that on the conventional chronology should date much earlier than Marathon, and the early date of the excavation hinders a detailed understanding of the stratigraphy that might have existed), virtually all scholars accept this mound as containing the grave of the Athenians. (For a short discussion of the various investigations of the mound that provides a good summary of the difficult nineteenth-century excavation reports as well as mentions of earlier finds on the Marathon plain and apparently in the mound, such as "Persian" arrowheads, see the comments of N. G. L. Hammond in an article that is primarily another contribution to the scholarly attempts to reconstruct the battle of Marathon and uses the position of the mound as part of the evidence: "The Campaign and the Battle of Marathon," *Journal of Hellenic Studies*, 1968, vol. 88, pp. 13–57; the mound is treated on pp. 14–18.) As an apparently closed deposit, the material from the mound should be dated by the latest objects that comprise it. The red-figure fragment is dated by the latest scholarship to the 490s BC by the conventional chronology (Cook, op. cit., p. 168, note 63, quoting Dyfri Williams; for the attribution of the fragment to the painter Onesimos and a short comment on the chronological implications, see now Dyfri Williams, "Onesimos and the Getty Iliupersis," *Greek Vases in the J. Paul Getty Museum, Volume 5*, Malibu, California, J. Paul Getty Museum, 1991, p. 44 and fig. 5). The small, black-figure oil vases (lekythoi) find close parallels in deposits in the Athenian Agora considered to belong to the Persian destruction. The Francis/Vickers position on the Marathon evidence is difficult to understand, for they have not addressed it in any detail. Apparently they believe that the bones do indeed belong to the 192 Athenian dead but that the mound was enlarged later under Cimon (possibly around 470 BC); the black-figure vases and the red-figure fragment thus belong to that time (Francis, op. cit., pp. 91, 134–5, note 82). How this would work in view of the stratigraphy that seems to show the lekythoi in close proximity, if not actually mixed, with the bones and ashes is unclear. In this case, new excavations in the mound might answer many questions, but, given the present nature of the mound as an historic monument, this is unlikely to happen. Other sites in Athens conventionally connected with the Persians could do with more study, such as the North Wall of the Acropolis and the Themistoklean city wall, which is considered, on the evidence of Thucydides (1.93), to have been erected hastily using reused material, including sculpture, immediately after the withdrawal of the Persians. Stretches of this wall have been found with conventionally dated pre-Persian sculpture built into its lower levels, which seems appropriate, but does not fit with the new chronology that requires them to date much later and to have been put into the wall during a rebuilding or strengthening. Further study of the wall has already been urged by Vickers in his *Numismatic Chronicle* article (op. cit., pp. 29–30).

Index